MOUNTAIN

OF

FIRE

The Eruption and Survivors of Mount St. Helens

Also by Rebecca E. F. Barone

Unbreakable:
The Spies Who Cracked the Nazis' Secret Code

Race to the Bottom of the Earth:
Surviving Antarctica

MOUNTAIN
OF
FIRE

The Eruption and Survivors
of Mount St. Helens

Rebecca E. F. Barone

HENRY HOLT AND COMPANY
NEW YORK

Henry Holt and Company, *Publishers since 1866*
Henry Holt® is a registered trademark of Macmillan Publishing Group, LLC
120 Broadway, New York, NY 10271 • mackids.com

Our books may be purchased in bulk for promotional, educational, or
business use. Please contact your local bookseller or the Macmillan
Corporate and Premium Sales Department at (800) 221-7945 ext. 5442
or by email at MacmillanSpecialMarkets@macmillan.com.

Library of Congress Cataloging-in-Publication Data
Names: Barone, Rebecca E. F., author.
Title: Mountain of fire : the eruption and survivors of
Mount St. Helens / Rebecca E.F. Barone.
Description: First edition. | New York : Henry Holt and Company, 2024. |
Includes bibliographical references and index. | Audience: Ages 10–14 |
Audience: Grades 7–9 | Summary: "Mountain of Fire is the narrative
nonfiction story of the violent volcanic eruption of Mount St. Helens on
May 18, 1980, the story of the people who died, those who survived, and the
heroes who fought to raise an alarm. For weeks, the ground around Mount
St. Helens shuddered like a dynamite keg ready to explode. There were
legends of previous eruptions: violent fire, treacherous floods, and heat that
had scoured the area. But the shaking and swelling was unlike any volcano
ever seen before. Day and night, scientists tried to piece together the mountain's
clues—yet nothing could prepare them for the destruction to come. The
long-dormant volcano seethed away, boiling rock far below the surface.
Washington's governor, Dixie Lee Ray, understood the despair that would
follow from people being forced from their homes. How and when should
she give orders to evacuate the area? And would that be enough to save the
people from the eruption of Mount St. Helens?"— Provided by publisher.
Identifiers: LCCN 2023030580 | ISBN 9781250881656 (hardcover)
Subjects: LCSH: Saint Helens, Mount (Wash.)—Eruption,
1980—Juvenile literature.
Classification: LCC QE523.S23 B37 2024 | DDC 551.2109797/84—dc23/
eng/20231116
LC record available at https://lccn.loc.gov/2023030580

First edition, 2024
Book design by Ellen Duda
Printed in the United States of America by Lakeside Book Company,
Harrisonburg, Virginia

ISBN 978-1-250-88165-6
1 3 5 7 9 10 8 6 4 2

To Adam and Lydia

To view photos of the people and places of this story, including the eruption and aftermath, please go to https://read.macmillan.com/mountain-of-fire/ or use the QR code below.

KEY PLACES

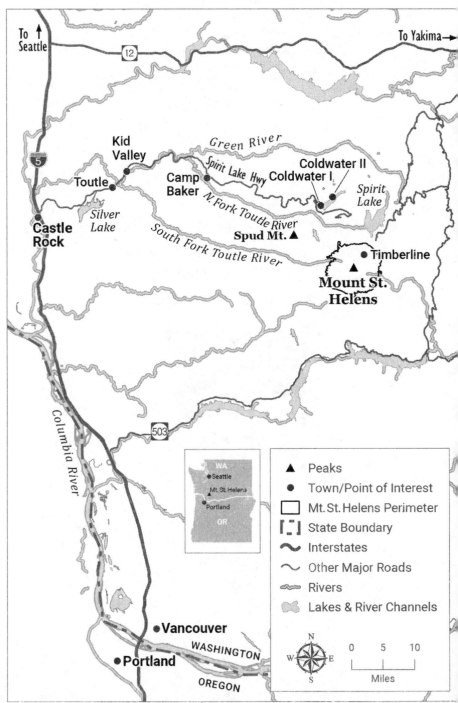

KEY PEOPLE

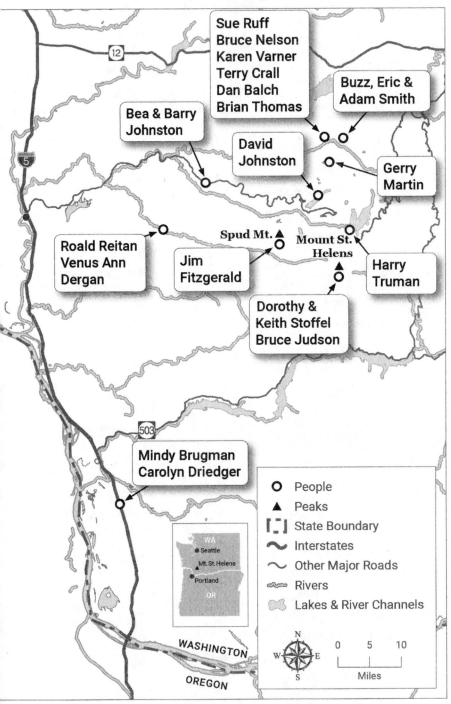

Sue Ruff
Bruce Nelson
Karen Varner
Terry Crall
Dan Balch
Brian Thomas

Buzz, Eric &
Adam Smith

Bea & Barry
Johnston

David
Johnston

Gerry
Martin

Roald Reitan
Venus Ann
Dergan

Spud Mt. ▲

Mount St.
Helens

Jim
Fitzgerald

Harry
Truman

Dorothy &
Keith Stoffel
Bruce Judson

Mindy Brugman
Carolyn Driedger

○ People
▲ Peaks
[ ] State Boundary
〜 Interstates
〜 Other Major Roads
〜 Rivers
░ Lakes & River Channels

WA
● Seattle
▲ Mt. St. Helens
● Portland
OR

WASHINGTON
OREGON

N
W E
S

0   5   10
Miles

TABLE OF CONTENTS

AUTHOR'S NOTE

I was fortunate to be able to interview many of the key figures in this book, and I am grateful for the time they shared with me.

Where I was not able to conduct interviews myself, and in some instances to round out the stories I did hear firsthand, I used interviews and accounts recorded in books, videos, and articles. Present-tense quotes taken from these sources have been transcribed to the past tense to better fit the narrative here.

CHARACTERS

Several figures appearing in this book have the same last name. To avoid confusion, scientists, reporters, and politicians are referred to by their last names, while those figures whose primary story takes place during the eruption are referred to by their first names.

Names used to identify each figure are underlined, and, unless noted, are all adults.

Scientists
USGS

Robert "Bob" Christiansen—*head of USGS*

Dwight "Rocky" Crandell—geologist/volcanologist

Carolyn Driedger—glaciologist

Harry Glicken—volcanologist

Steve Hodge—glaciologist

David A. Johnston—volcanologist

Mark Meier—glaciologist

Dan Miller—geologist

Jim Moore—volcanologist

Donal "Don" Mullineaux—geologist/volcanologist

Don Swanson—volcanologist

Richard Waitt—volcanologist

Randy White—seismologist

University of Washington

Steve Malone—seismologist

Linda Noson—seismic analyst

Pennsylvania State University

Barry <u>Voight</u>—landslide expert

California Institute of Technology

Mindy <u>Brugman</u>—glaciologist

University of Wikato

Janine <u>Krippner</u>—volcanologist

Politicians

Governor Dixy Lee <u>Ray</u>—governor of Washington State

Ray <u>Walters</u>—Governor Ray's press secretary

Weyerhaeuser Logging Company

Jim <u>Rombach</u>—Forest Engineer and Safety Officer

Jack <u>Schoening</u>—Woods Manager

James <u>Scymanky</u>—logger

Reporters

Donna <u>duBeth</u>—journalist

Roger <u>Werth</u>—photographer

Around the mountain

Ferrol <u>Fullmer</u>—hotel manager

Harry <u>Truman</u>—owner of Spirit Lake Lodge

Otto <u>Sieber</u>—adventurer

Andy Sterne—adventurer

Brian Witt—adventurer

Duane Rhodes—Boy Scout leader

Jack Wolff—YMCA leader

Gerry Martin—citizen scientist

Jim Fitzgerald—geology student

Bea Johnston—geology student

Barry Johnston—husband of Bea Johnston

Adam Smith—camper, seven years old

Edwin "Buzz" Smith—logger

Eric Smith—camper, ten years old

Sue Ruff—camper

Bruce Nelson—camper

Terry Crall—camper

Karen Varner—camper

Dan Balch—camper

Brian Thomas—camper

Grant Christiansen—veteran

Venus Ann Dergan—camper

Roald Reitan—camper

Rescue workers

Michael Cooney—pararescue jumper

Major Mike Peters—pilot

Law enforcement

Washington State Patrol

Captain Dick Bullock

Chief Robert Landon

County officers

Bill Closner—Skamania County Sheriff

Les Nelson—Cowlitz County Sheriff

PROLOGUE

THE MORNING WAS CALM, QUIET. THE SKY WAS CLEAR. FIVE AND a half miles in the distance, Mount St. Helens rose to a snow-covered peak.

Five and a half miles sounded far. Five and a half miles might seem like safety.

But David Johnston knew better. He knew volcanoes. He knew their speed. Five and a half miles, he knew, would never be enough.

Johnston was in the clearing, tending to the scientific instruments and radios, for one night only.

Maybe, he hoped, the mountain would stay quiet.

There was work to do. Measurements to take. Data to record. And, always, the mountain to watch. To be ready to raise the first alarm.

He was watching at 8:32 a.m.

Without warning, without a hint of noise, the side of the mountain fell away. The gray mass of roiling earth began tumbling, rolling down and away from the summit. A landslide that seconds later was followed by another.

Then, a blast. Darker, choppier.

Faster.

Johnston grabbed for the radio. He clicked it on. "Vancouver! Vancouver!" he said, breathlessly. "This is it!"

He clicked the microphone once more. And again.

Then, silence.

The gray, frothing blast swept toward him.

Five and a half miles would never be far enough.

MARCH 20–27, 1980

CHAPTER 1

59 Days Before the Eruption

THE THICK METAL CYLINDER TURNED SLOWLY. DAY AND NIGHT, it guided a long, narrow piece of paper moving faithfully underneath a quivering black pen. Day and night, the pen drew an unbroken, straight line.

Until 3:47 p.m.

Far underneath the surface of the earth, rock tore away from rock as a giant slab of the earth's crust wrested free from its trap. The earth trembled at the tear.

Miles above, the pen that had been steady a moment before jumped to life.

In a basement lab at the University of Washington in Seattle, Linda Noson was the first to notice. She knew as soon as she saw the dark marks streaking across the face of the paper: an earthquake. A big one.

Noson ran upstairs.

"We just got a four," she told Steve Malone, the head of the seismology lab. "From the Mount Rainier station."

Malone was up and out of his office the same moment. In the Pacific Northwest, there were thousands of earthquakes each year. But few reached as high as a magnitude 4.

The seismometer on Mount Rainer had registered the earthquake, but that didn't mean the center of the quake was anywhere near. Seismometers could detect movement of the earth's crust far from where the instruments were actually located. There had been an earthquake out there—somewhere—but where?

"I bet it's Mount Hood," said a student who had joined Noson and Malone.

"I'm thinking it's St. Helens," countered Malone, his intuition coming from years working around the mountains.

There was only one way to tell.

Noson was a seismic analyst, an expert in examining the lines and lurches of the recorder's pen. Straight or jagged, the recorder showed only a black path. Like all of science, it needed humans to translate the data into a meaningful story. Noson went to work.

Taking the paper, she noted times, locations, and magnitudes of movement. She went to her computer and wrote some code, walked a set of punch cards to the mainframe in another building, and waited while it slugged through the calculations.

"Steve's right," she said when she walked back into Malone's office. "It's Mount St. Helens."

A call to the Forest Service ranger station on Mount St. Helens confirmed it. Everyone there had felt the quake.

One earthquake—even a big earthquake—could be shaken off. One earthquake, alone, wasn't much to worry about.

As long as it was only one.

But over the night and into the next day, the earthquakes didn't stop.

It had been an ordinary, unremarkable Thursday afternoon when the first earthquake rolled the ground. Now the peace was broken.

Malone began to worry about avalanches. There was fresh snow on the ground, and Mount St. Helens was popular with mountain climbers. It might be time to get everyone off the mountain.

But when Malone called the avalanche forecaster to update him on the earthquakes, there was a different question weighing on the forecaster's mind. They all knew stories of how Mount St. Helens had erupted in the past. Ash had clogged the sky, turning bright day to black midnight. Pumice had rained down. Fire and lava had spewed from the summit. The Toutle River had become so hot that all the fish had died for miles around the mountain. It had happened barely more than a century before.

It could happen again.

"Is there going to be an eruption?" the forecaster asked.

"Well," Malone replied, "we don't know. But these earthquakes are continuing. So, sometime. Maybe. There could."

All weekend, the ground trembled and danced. "Sometime" seemed to grow closer every time the earth shook.

✹

By Monday, Malone was beginning to panic.

Malone knew seismology. He knew the signs and signals of moving rock. What he didn't understand were volcanoes.

Luckily, he knew someone who did.

Dwight "Rocky" Crandell and his field partner Donal "Don" Mullineaux were volcanologists who had spent more than two decades studying Mount St. Helens with the United States Geological Survey (USGS). They had often traveled to Washington from their home base in Denver, Colorado, and they knew the mountain well. If something was about to happen, if Mount St. Helens was showing signs of erupting, they would know.

But when Malone first called Crandell to ask him for advice, Crandell's response was hardly what he was expecting.

"Don't worry. Don't worry, Steve," Crandell said. "The national [seismometer] network located it, and [the earthquake] is thirty kilometers [18.6 miles] away. Not a problem."

Malone was shocked.

"Woah! Rocky! Hang on. Wait a minute," Malone exclaimed. "We've got a station right at the volcano, on the west flank. And another one about fifty kilometers [31 miles] away . . . Our locations might be off by one or two kilometers [0.6 or 1.2 miles], but not thirty [18.6 miles]!"

Malone's instruments were much closer to Mount St. Helens than the USGS's network; after that first earthquake the week before, Malone had put seismometers *directly on* the mountain. Malone's instruments, and Malone's records, were the most reliable sources of information. To Crandell, the earthquakes appeared too far away for concern; to Malone, it seemed like Crandell was looking at bad data.

"There is no question," continued Malone, "that this earthquake is located directly under the volcano, slightly to the north of the summit, and at a very shallow depth!"

Slowly, Malone convinced Crandell that the earthquakes were indeed coming from Mount St. Helens. And they were coming faster and stronger every day.

"That got his attention," Malone remembered.

Crandell had a project in Denver that he couldn't leave, but his field partner, Mullineaux, was in Washington State the next day.

It was a good thing Mullineaux had come quickly, too. Because on Tuesday night, the earthquake activity increased tremendously. Noson had run up to Malone's office for a single magnitude 4 earthquake. Now, there were several magnitude 4 earthquakes *per hour*.

It's going somewhere, Malone thought to himself.

By Wednesday, the earthquakes were coming even faster. So many strong earthquakes, continuing for so many days, meant that something was going to happen.

"Well," said Malone, "the next day, it did."

CHAPTER 2

A KEG OF DYNAMITE

"IT SOUNDED JUST LIKE A SONIC BOOM," SAID FERROL FULLMER, who managed a hotel nearby.

At 12:58 p.m. on Thursday, March 27, 1980—one week after earthquakes had begun shaking the mountain—a plume of ash and steam shot seven thousand feet into the air from the top of Mount St. Helens.

On the ground, people stared up and wondered at the noise, but they couldn't see anything. Clouds covered the mountain's summit.

"People got on the roofs of buildings for a better view, but it just looked like a lot of black rain clouds," said Fullmer.

They heard the boom. They knew that the mountain had been shaking. But to people below the clouds, Mount St. Helens looked like it did any other day.

"There was no sign of molten lava," one newspaper reported, sounding somewhat frustrated.

Not only was there no lava, there was no surge of hot gases rushing down the mountainside. There were no mudflows cascading through the river. There was no ash falling like misplaced snow.

"Mount St. Helens, a lady with a 123-year-old tummyache, erupted with a gigantic volcanic burp," the *Spokesman-Review* wrote, condescendingly.

And just like a burp, the plume died off after it made some noise.

If this is what the earthquakes had been leading to, well, everyone was a bit disappointed. A loud "boom" . . . and that was it. A burp, even a big one, was hardly anything to get upset about.

The clouds made it especially easy to dismiss the steam blast. The only way to see the top of the mountain was to take to the air, and soon, the sky above the summit was full of planes.

It was exciting! It was thrilling! A volcano! There didn't *seem* to be any danger. The plume subsided after its initial eruption, and it was a beautiful day. Who wouldn't want to go see a once-in-more-than-a-hundred-years eruption?

"Dozens of light aircraft, filled with sightseers, journalists, geologists and even the governor—all eager for a peek at a real live volcano, flew through mostly clear skies [above the clouds] surrounding Mt. St. Helens Thursday afternoon," reported the *Spokesman-Review*.

Even Governor Dixy Lee Ray hadn't been concerned when she first heard about the eruption. In nearby Port Ludlow, she had been meeting with the judges of Washington State's Supreme Court when she was interrupted.

"I might just read you the note that has just been handed to me," she said, smiling. "We have received information that Mount St. Helens has erupted at 12:58 today," she continued. "I've always said, for many years, that I hoped I lived long enough to see one of our volcanoes erupt. Maybe I soon will get a chance."

She flew to Mount St. Helens that afternoon.

When her plane landed after circling the top of the volcano, she told the assembled reporters that "we could not see any steam or lava . . . from what we could see, everything is quiet now." Still, she agreed that "it was really quite a thrill."

To the audience in the sky, it seemed like the mountain-turned-volcano was the best event of the season—something to enjoy and not be scared of. But these were tourists. None of them had experience with volcanoes.

There was only one man in the sky that afternoon who had seen an eruption before. He had just happened to be in the area when the earthquakes had started; he had stayed to study what was coming next. David Johnston had a feeling that Mount St. Helens wasn't done yet.

Johnston was a volcanologist with experience in active volcanoes in Alaska. As a scientist for the USGS, he was usually based in California, but he had been attending a conference in Seattle when the earthquakes began. Over the past week, Malone had put Johnston to work deciphering seismic signals, but Johnston's specialty was volcanic gases. Now, with the mountain spewing steam and ash, he could really put his knowledge to work.

On the afternoon of the first blast from Mount St. Helens, Johnston stood in a clearing near the forest with his hands stuffed in his pockets. His shaggy, blond hair was caught under a blue knit winter hat, and his checkered flannel coat guarded him from the winter weather that still chilled the air in late March. An easy grin played across his face as he slouched and faced the reporters.

No one would've guessed that Johnston hated speaking in front of a crowd. He was so afraid of public speaking that, more than once, he had fainted while giving presentations.

But that fear paled next to the deal the reporters had offered: a view of Mount St. Helens from the sky, in exchange for an on-camera interview.

It was enough to make him smile, even in front of a crowd. Johnston swallowed his fear and climbed aboard the plane.

In the air, they followed the winding path of a river, over the old-growth forests blanketing the landscape below. While they flew beneath the clouds, bare, brown patches of ground were visible where the Weyerhaeuser Logging Company had harvested timber on some of the most profitable land in the country. Soon, though, Johnston and the news crew were rising above the clouds, finally catching sight of the top of the mountain.

The peak of Mount St. Helens, usually pristine with snow, was scarred with gray ash. As they drew closer, the ash resolved into cracks and crevasses, streaking down an otherwise blank, white mountain.

In the plane, every pair of eyes followed the gray lines up. There, at the top of the mountain, they saw it for the first time. A new crater.

"This is 335," one of the crew said over the radio, announcing their flight number before reporting what he saw. "I've got a bit of steam coming out of it, and I'd say it's probably about, uh, a twelve-hundred-foot crater. It's open at the very top of the mountain. About twelve-hundred feet by, about, oh, perhaps two hundred feet in the center."

Long gashes, like wounds in the earth from some terrified beast clawing at a nightmare, raked the ground next to the crater on the mountain top.

"We've got a crater," one of the crew said again. "It appears to just be slowly developing all across the top."

They circled Mount St. Helens and watched as a small landslide opened the crater a bit wider.

When they came down after the flight, the reporters asked: What did Johnston think? Were the plume of steam and the slowly growing crater the end of the mountain's drama, or was there more to come? The crowd of tourists in planes seemed to be having a good time, enjoying the spectacle from the air. But what was the real story?

Were the people of Mount St. Helens in danger?

"We're standing next to a dynamite keg and the fuse is lit," said Johnston. "I am genuinely afraid of it."

LATE MARCH–MAY 16, 1980

CHAPTER 3

THE ONE WHO SMOKES

JOHNSTON SHOULD *NOT* HAVE COMPARED THE MOUNTAIN TO A keg of dynamite. That was the last thing the US Geological Survey (USGS) needed: People were going to panic if they heard stories like that.

"We don't know how this will play out," a senior USGS scientist chided Johnston. "We don't want people in harm's way but [we] can't be fright merchants."

They were scientists, and their story should be grounded in theory, not guesses.

"There's really no good way to predict what will happen. No way," Don Mullineaux told reporters.

And no one knew the volcanic science of Mount St. Helens better than Rocky Crandell and Don Mullineaux.

The USGS monitored the country's volcanic hazards, and Mullineaux and Crandell were in charge of the Cascades, a mountain range in western North America. They were geologists who specialized in mapping previous eruptions. They'd used the records laid down in rock and dirt over centuries and millennia to weave a story of what had happened long ago.

"When I first met [Crandell]," Steve Malone remembered,

thinking back to years before when the two crossed paths around Mount St. Helens, "he was really fit looking, with all of his geology stuff hanging off of him . . . he had the holster for the rock hammer, and the notebooks, and the cameras . . . outfitted with all the gear."

Crandell, and Mullineaux with him, dug through layers of rock and soil, seeing how ash from previous eruptions changed the ground. They hiked over ridges and down valleys, searching to see how far each layer of ash stretched away from the mountain. They watched the trees and banks of the rivers. Where the Toutle River branched into the North Fork and the South Fork, they found that lahars—mudslides like thick cement containing everything from ice and dirt to trees and rocks moving as fast as 120 miles an hour—had flowed down each.

In their final report, Crandell and Mullineaux wrote that "Mount St. Helens has been more active and more explosive during the last 4,500 years than any other volcano in the conterminous United States."

"The volcano's behavior suggests . . . an eruption is more likely to occur within the next hundred years, and perhaps even before the end of this century," they concluded.

A few newspapers, mainly around Washington, picked up the story and wrote about the volcanologists who sounded "a little gleeful," according to one.

But most journalists seemed unimpressed by the volcanologists' predictions.

"Two experts say St. Helens could erupt before the end of the century. They're right. It could erupt next week or wait 500 years," another article offered.

Crandell and Mullineaux's report was full of mights, maybes, and perhapses. According to the two scientists, it was impossible to exactly predict anything, and the volcano seemed capable of doing everything . . . or nothing.

The report was circulated and then filed away.

But Crandell and Mullineaux were far from the first to realize that Mount St. Helens had a long history of eruptions. Stories and traditions of the mountain's violence had been passed down for centuries.

The Upper Cowlitz people native to the land called the volcano "Lawillayt-łá: one who smokes," while the Puyallup people named it "Loowit" or "Lady of Fire." European explorers had renamed it Mount St. Helens, in honor of Alleyne FitzHerbert, 1st Baron St. Helens, a British ambassador to Spain. They could rename it, but no amount of European influence could dim the legendary eruptions.

One story from the Klickitat tribe, recorded in 1853, told how Mount St. Helens and Mount Hood, which stood sixty miles southeast, "were man and wife; they quarreled and threw fire at one another, and Mount St. Helens was the victor." But that wasn't the only conclusion they drew; the Klickitat tribe didn't feel that the story had ended. Since their fight, "Mount Hood had been afraid, while St. Helens, having a stout heart, still burns."

There were stories of eruptions in 1781, 1799, 1800, and many times between 1831 and 1853. Legends told how ash spewing from the summit would blanket the ground for miles. Fishermen reported that eruptions caused the Toutle River to grow hot enough to kill fish.

But all of that was known only through stories. The last eruption—around 125 years before Crandell and Mullineaux's report—was long before any modern scientific record. The only information that the volcanologists had to go on was what the rocks themselves and the handed-down stories could tell them.

But the "one who smokes" would not lie quiet forever.

Crandell and Mullineaux's report had dire words couched between their cautious predictions.

"We believe [Mount St. Helens] to be an especially dangerous volcano," they wrote. "In the future Mount St. Helens probably will erupt violently and affect human life, property, and economic welfare . . ."

Just when, though, neither Crandell nor Mullineaux could say.

CHAPTER 4

PROBLEMS WITH THE PRESS

THE FIRST ERUPTION—THE SMALLISH BLAST OF STEAM AND ASH from the new crater—quickly subsided. Other little "burps" followed, all disappearing just as quickly. The earthquakes continued.

Was this it? Were these small eruptions and intermittent earthquakes the whole of Mount St. Helens's show? Or, were these simply the warm-up for whatever was coming next? The more the mountain shook, the more people demanded answers.

Crandell, Mullineaux, and another USGS scientist named Dan Miller ran press conferences that swelled with every new movement of the mountain.

"Holy smokes!" a representative from the National Forest headquarters said when he first stepped into the room of reporters. "You'd think the *President's* coming!"

"Let's not beat around the bush," one reporter demanded when Mullineaux sat down at another conference. "When'll it blow? How bad?"

"I can't tell *if* it will erupt," Mullineaux replied, "let alone how or when."

"This nation can put a man on the moon, but *you* can't tell us if the volcano will erupt?"

"That's right!" Mullineaux replied, exasperated.

He had good reason to be frustrated, too; some of the questions he faced bordered on the ridiculous. At one press conference, a reporter chimed in wanting to know about the snow-covered sides of the mountain and the glaciers at the top.

"Wouldn't melting snow extinguish the volcano?" the reporter asked.

"Well, no . . . heh, heh," Mullineaux responded as he tried to stifle a laugh. "Surely not."

Crandell, Mullineaux, and Miller ran the official USGS press conferences, but there were so many voices—scientific voices with advanced degrees—that it was hard to keep straight what the best truth was.

Even Johnston couldn't stop from giving reporters dramatic predictions. He had been scolded for comparing the mountain to dynamite, but still reporters quoted him saying that Mount St. Helens will "just go *Bang!* Magma will come up from however deep, maybe no warning before the big eruption."

Like the tourists who had flooded to the newly awake volcano, scientists had come, eager to see the spectacle, too.

A sixty-six-year-old Franco-Belgian named Haroun Tazieff who had once been the director of France's global physics institute showed up in early April with no warning. He demanded to be taken to the top of the mountain. His request was quickly denied, but the degrees surrounding his name were enough to gather a crowd of reporters.

"Significant eruption unlikely," he proclaimed, despite the absence of data supporting his conclusion.

Other voices chimed in—from the head of the University of Oregon's volcanology department, from Stanford University, and others—to counteract Johnston's drama. No, they agreed, Mount St. Helens was nothing to worry about.

The official voice of the USGS came from Crandell, Mullineaux, and Miller, three times a day. And, daily, the reporters couldn't quite decide what to make of them. In quiet, calming tones, Crandell, Mullineaux, and Miller talked about destruction blanketing the land for miles around the mountain. They gave evidence how eruptions thousands and hundreds of years ago had devastated the area. But they couldn't seem to tell anyone what level of danger they were actually in right now. And their manner and tone of voice seemed so peaceful. It was hard to reconcile their voice with their words.

"I'd give them fact, but [the reporters] wanted predictions," Mullineaux said. "To me, they wanted things that scientists could not do."

❋

The USGS was calm: They were not forecasting any major, imminent eruption, and the area around the mountain should be safe.

They believed their words.

By mid-April, the snow melted enough that snowplows could

clear a path on old logging roads up to a landing above Coldwater Creek. It was eight and a half miles northwest from the peak of Mount St. Helens, up a ridge more than 5,700 feet tall. With easy viewing to the summit of the volcano, yet down off its flanks and miles away from the erupting crater, Crandell established his team at this outpost. They named it Coldwater, after the creek directly below.

The conditions were sparse: They set up a tent, added radios, logbooks, and cameras, and positioned a scientist there around the clock.

At the Coldwater site, the only signs in the rock of previous eruptions were pieces of pumice (volcanic rock that fell from the sky) from 3,500 years before. Sheltering from pumice would've been an adventure, but it was survivable. Crandell and Mullineaux hadn't found any indication that a deadly cloud of hot gas erupting from Mount St. Helens in the past 4,500 years had ever made it up to this ledge.

If they couldn't see any sign that it had been harmed in the past, then that should mean it was safe in 1980.

Right?

CHAPTER 5

Caught in the Middle

THE SCIENTISTS STAYED AROUND THE MOUNTAIN, AND THE Weyerhaeuser loggers stayed, too. For the loggers, the mountain was their livelihood.

The loggers had all felt the earthquakes. March 27 had been a normal day at work when they heard the "boom!" of ash and steam exploding out of the new crater. Officials from Weyerhaeuser had sent the loggers home that day; the company had wanted them far from the mountain.

But since then, though the plumes hadn't stopped, one company official reported, "There's no concern of any immediate danger at all." So the loggers went back to their jobs, turning trees into the lumber that would build America.

The day after the first plume, the same news crew that had flown David Johnston to the peak of the mountain came again to Mount St. Helens. This time, however, they came to speak to the loggers, not to scientists.

Outside the Weyerhaeuser office, a logger sat in a yellow pickup truck, waiting to make his way into the forest to meet up with his team. When the reporter approached him and asked what he thought of the quakes and the ash and the steam issuing from the new crater, the logger didn't hesitate.

"Far as we know, it's a joke," he replied. "Could last a hundred years. We're going to stay until the rocks start fallin', I guess."

All the loggers seemed to feel the same way. They didn't think the mountain would make any more fuss.

At a work site, where loggers toasted bread over a campfire and sat on felled trees and rocks, the reporter tried again:

"You don't mind working in the shadow of the mountain?" he asked.

"No, not at all. There's nothing to be scared of," a logger replied.

But underneath them, the ground shook.

❇

Forest Engineer and Safety Officer Jim Rombach was in charge of making plans to keep the loggers safe in the event of a big eruption. He called Mullineaux for information.

"Eruptions will probably come slowly," Mullineaux said. It wasn't ash or gases that he advised Rombach to be wary of, but the floods and lahars. "Mud could drown the valley floors. Go uphill."

"How far?" Rombach asked.

"Thirty feet above the river. Mud can flow faster than people walk. But with radios you'll know."

So Weyerhaeuser mapped escape routes to high ground. They didn't have to rely on the main roads, either; their loggers knew the network of private roads they'd built through the trees. Mullineaux told them it would be enough to keep safe if they moved uphill; Weyerhaeuser officials made plans according to what they heard.

But what the Weyerhaeuser staff couldn't plan for were the other people—tourists—in the forest besides their loggers. Crandell, Mullineaux, and Miller repeated the danger three times a day at their press conferences. But still, some people insisted on coming to see the shaking, spewing mountain anyway.

People were starting to be a more immediate danger than the volcano next door.

CHAPTER 6

AN ERUPTION OF TOURISTS

FROM THE MOMENT THE MOUNTAIN STARTED PUFFING, MOUNT St. Helens had become a tourist attraction. The towns nearest the volcano began selling souvenirs, like bumper stickers that read "Lava or Leave It," and T-shirts that said "Mt. St. Helens, we lava you!"

The people were making a dangerous situation even worse.

"Tourists on our roads don't know logging," complained Jack Schoening, the woods manager of Weyerhaeuser. "They stop in the roads and block log trucks. They must be stopped."

Law enforcement was trying.

When the mountain first began erupting on March 27, three county deputies were sent to staff a roadblock at the line between Skamania and Cowlitz counties, just west of the mountain. It was a good idea—they were trying to keep people away from what could be a very dangerous situation. Unfortunately, it didn't work as well as they wanted.

In the first place, the roadblock kept moving. There wasn't a clear definition of the line between "safe" and "dangerous."

And even when the roadblock stayed in place for a few hours, it was possible to get around it if you knew the right people. When

Donna duBeth, a reporter for the Longview *Daily News*, first tried to get through, two deputies pulled her over.

"No one passes," one said. He gestured to crews from NBC, CBS, and *Time* magazine. "You can join the big boys over there."

"And *you* can step aside," duBeth retorted. "Here's a note from the sheriff."

She went through.

It was a mess. The roadblock was hardly secure.

And people just kept coming!

Journalists came. News crews with cameras and more reporters came. And as the days passed and people learned that papers and magazines were willing to pay for any clean shot of the smoldering volcano, the ridges began filling with tourists waiting and waiting for clouds to lift so they could snap a picture.

"When the weather was clear," one Washington Emergency Services staffer reported, "the road up to the mountain looked like downtown Seattle at rush hour."

It wasn't just the roads that were attracting traffic, either. On one afternoon, there were an incredible *seventy* aircraft full of media and tourists—in addition to the helicopters and planes the scientists used—circling the mountain.

People even came to the ash-spewing summit itself. A mere six days after it first started erupting, a newspaper ran a picture of a young man who had climbed to the rim of the crater and back down. They printed his picture under the headline: IT'S EXCITING AND FUN: HAWKERS, GAWKERS JAM ROADS.

Others came to sell a story through somewhat more dubious

means. Otto Sieber, Brian Witt, and Andy Sterne hired a helicopter to take them to the top of Mount St. Helens with film and camera equipment. But that wasn't all they brought; they also came bearing beer. As the volcano shot a spectacular burst of ash and gas two thousand feet into the air, Sieber took a picture of Witt popping the tab on a beer can and blowing foam into the wind. They repeated the whole thing with another brand of beer minutes later.

"I don't consider this illegal," Sieber said. "We're documenting natural history."

Admittedly, they hoped that the beer companies would pay a high price for their documents of natural history à la beer can. One sold picture, they figured, would cover the cost of the helicopter.

The press ate it up. Mount St. Helens was news.

There was no one set to stand out more as a character of the mountain than Harry Truman (no relation to the former president of the United States).

Truman had run the Mount St. Helens Lodge for fifty years. Six miles from the mountain, on the edge of Spirit Lake—a lake created thousands of years before when another eruption had dammed the Toutle River—Harry and his wife, Edie, had hosted tourists and run their store from the green, wooden building nestled in the trees. The lodge had been a labor of love and a project they ran together.

In the spring of 1980, it had been three years since Edie had died, and Harry hadn't handled it well. He never seemed to be without a drink in his hand—Coke and whiskey, no matter the time of day. The lodge had become mired in disrepair. Harry had acquired sixteen cats, but he didn't take care of them; the most frequent comment that reporters and tourists had upon leaving the lodge was that it stank of cat urine.

But to Harry, the lodge was where he and Edie had lived their lives.

Donna duBeth made her way to Truman's home a few days after Mount St. Helens began to erupt.

"A UW [University of Washington] seismologist says earth-quakes can lead to eruption," she told Truman.

"I've felt no earthquakes and there'll be no eruption," was Truman's emphatic reply. "I'm gonna stay till hell freezes over."

Donna duBeth's article ran under the headline GIVE 'EM HELL, HARRY, and she quoted him saying "I'm the king of Spirit Lake. I stuck it out fifty-four years. I'm gonna stay."

It was a sentiment he repeated to the other reporters who came to visit.

"What [do] you think of the earthquakes?" one reporter asked.

"Haven't felt a quiver. Wouldn't even know if I weren't asked to yak to TV cameras," said Harry.

"The Forest Service just shut the mountain. You going to leave?"

"Naw. I've got the best little resort in the whole U-S-A. They're not gonna get me off this mountain. And if the [expletive deleted] blows, I'm the only one up there."

He toned down his language as much as he was able to for

the *Today* show and responded to questions about the mountain dangerously erupting by saying "That's just poop."

The press had found their star in the blunt old man determined to stay by his mountain.

Harry Truman loved Mount St. Helens, but the scientists were the ones determined to understand what was coming. At any cost.

CHAPTER 7

THE BEST OF SIGNS, THE WORST OF SIGNS

DON SWANSON SPENT HIS FIRST HOURS AT MOUNT ST. HELENS leaning out of a hovering helicopter directly over the summit of the volcano.

The mountain was still intermittently belching steam and ash, and the best record of what was going on *inside* the volcano was the elements that came spewing *up*, out the top. Getting close enough to reach a sample, however, meant reaching into the mouth of the beast.

They timed it as best they could to swoop down between bursts. Using a soup ladle attached to an ice axe, Swanson reached out, straining to touch the ground as the helicopter lowered nearer and nearer the summit. He scooped out a serving of hot ash and quickly pulled himself back inside.

Safely down in the lab, Swanson and his team found that the ash was old rock—there was no indication of new magma erupting out from deep inside the earth.

That was a very good sign.

The old rock seemed to say that Mount St. Helens was simply letting off steam, not preparing to blow its top.

But the scientists weren't content with just one conclusion; they were using every tool within reach to try to figure out what the mountain was up to.

For the moment, David Johnston had a safer job than Swanson. Johnston's specialty was volcanic gases, and he could examine those from a distance. From the Coldwater site and another site, named Timberline, directly on the mountain, Johnston peered through a big, boxy instrument called a correlation spectrometer. By looking through it, Johnston could observe how much sulfur dioxide (SO_2) was coming from the mountain. He had found on other volcanoes that the release of SO_2 sometimes signaled that an eruption was nearing.

When he examined the plume from Mount St. Helens, Johnston barely detected SO_2.

That was another very good sign.

The mountain might be making noise, but from these measurements, it didn't seem like it would end up making too much of a fuss.

Farther away, in his basement lab at the University of Washington in Seattle, however, Steve Malone was beginning to feel certain that the conclusions from Swanson's and Johnston's work were wrong.

On the evening of April 3, Malone was back in his lab, showing seismometer data to Randy White. White was part of the USGS team from Menlo Park, California. They were in Washington to help try to predict the volcano's next move.

Malone and White were looking at the recorders when the pens began to fly across the paper.

And they didn't stop.

"Oh my gosh!" White exclaimed. "The volcano is erupting right now!"

Malone and White rushed to the phone to call the Forest Service. They had a plane above the mountain almost twenty-four hours a day.

"Nope!" the pilot responded, when they reached him. "Everything's all quiet. Nothing's going on."

"Wow . . ." White breathed out a sigh of mixed relief and disbelief. "I have never seen this strong a volcanic tremor other than when a volcano's erupting," he told Malone.

But no, the Forest Service had eyes on the volcano. No, it was not erupting.

Yet White was right to be worried. The seismometer didn't lie. He and Malone had just witnessed something big. This was a new type of earthquake at Mount St. Helens: a harmonic tremor.

Most earthquakes occur when sections of the earth's crust far below the surface rub up against one another, get stuck, and then jerk free all at once. On the surface, people feel that jerk of release as an earthquake.

"The assumption with the large earthquake," Malone explained, "is that it's a fracture of the rock . . . Like if you bend a stick and it breaks, you hear a pop—that's the earthquake!"

Those kinds of earthquakes had been occurring around and beneath Mount St. Helens since March 20. The rock underneath the mountain was jerking and breaking and moving. It happened many times, but each tremor was finished in a matter of seconds.

Then, on March 31, the ground under Mount St. Helens rolled for a full two minutes without stopping. The next day, April 1, it shook for five.

"This type of tremor came and went, off and on," remembered Malone. "We really couldn't figure out what [triggered it]. Sometimes it would start when an earthquake occurred, and then it would keep rumbling. Sometimes it would just come out of the background . . . going on for several minutes and then quit. And other times, an earthquake [would begin], and it would stop. Sometimes, there was an earthquake in the middle. There was no pattern that we could discern."

Unlike the larger earthquakes, where scientists had a single, generally accepted theory about what was happening far below the surface, there were several theories about what caused harmonic tremors.

"Personally, I think, what it is, is many tiny earthquakes one right after another," said Malone. "Rather than the ground slipping—kabam!—it slowly kind of inches along [during a harmonic tremor]. Very much like the horrible screech you hear when chalk rubs against a chalkboard."

It could slowly slide along, because instead of being solid, the rock of a harmonic tremor was fluid. This wasn't hard rock against hard rock; harmonic tremors were earthquakes of solid rock against magma, "like squishy rock sliding on solid rock," explained Malone.

These were entirely different types of earthquakes than what had come before. These tremors predicted something far more dire.

Magma was on the move.

When Rocky Crandell heard about the change in earthquakes, he was momentarily stunned. There was fear in his voice when he muttered, "How can all this tremor *not* lead to an eruption?"

CHAPTER 8

THE BULGE

IF MAGMA WAS MOVING, WHERE WAS IT GOING?

Other than his initial ice-axe-and-soup-ladle science, Don Swanson's job was geodetic monitoring, which meant very accurately measuring and analyzing the size and shape of the earth. Usually, the earth changes slowly. The Himalayan mountains rise about a third of an inch per year—fingernails grow more than twice as fast. But right before a volcano erupts, the ground around it sometimes grows dramatically.

At Swanson's home lab in Hawaii, the volcanoes Kīlauea and Mauna Loa were like blisters, rising as magma swelled inside and then deflating once the fluid was released in an eruption. Now, coming to Washington and Mount St. Helens, Swanson guessed that this volcano would swell before it erupted, too. Perhaps by examining the ground around Mount St. Helens, the scientists would be able to predict a big eruption and give everyone a warning.

For a week, Swanson watched and measured the rocky top of the mountain. For an entire week, the exposed mountainside barely moved. Mount St. Helens didn't seem to be swelling.

It was a good sign.

Or it would have been a good sign, if it were true.

Swanson was looking in the wrong place.

It wasn't until the beginning of April that anyone began to look at Goat Rocks.

Back in the 1800s, a lava dome called Goat Rocks had formed about two thousand feet below the summit. Rising in jagged punches toward the sky, it had marked the landscape of Mount St. Helens for as long as modern scientists had been studying it. They knew it well.

They *had* known it well.

During his first days at Mount St. Helens, Swanson had flown to Goat Rocks and Sugar Bowl, another feature on the mountain about fifteen hundred feet below Goat Rocks. At each site, he had secured large boards painted bright orange onto the rock. Nailed together to form an X, Swanson could easily see these targets from far away.

On Sunday, April 13, three miles from the mountain's summit at the Timberline observation station, Swanson peered through a theodolite, an instrument that measured angles very accurately.

The orange boards seemed to shimmer and sway in the sun's heat, confusing Swanson's view and making it difficult to record measurements. Swanson gradually adjusted to the environment, so unlike the volcanoes he was used to in Hawaii. Slowly, precisely, he marked down angles and distances.

Sugar Bowl didn't move. He was certain of it. The rocks of that formation stayed put.

But as Swanson took more measurements over the course of an

hour and a half, Goat Rocks seemed to crawl away from him by a full twelve inches.

These numbers can't be real, he thought. *Volcanoes don't move this much.*

Swanson had expected to use small, almost imperceptible changes of the earth to predict the eruption of Mount St. Helens. Even the fastest spots on Kīlauea didn't move several inches in a matter of hours.

Swanson was stunned. He had never seen swelling like this before.

The area around Goat Rocks was bulging at an unbelievable rate. And it had been growing for days. Or weeks.

Just as Swanson made his discovery, Crandell and Mullineaux approached the Timberline parking lot. They hadn't been out to see the mountain since the first days of the volcano's blasts skyward. They had been trapped at the USGS offices in Vancouver, trying to weave a story that balanced caution and terror. But now, at Timberline, they looked at the mountain, at the rocks and snow and trees they had been used to seeing for decades, and they were aghast.

"I had no idea how the mountain's changed," Crandell said as he looked at Goat Rocks. "It's way too steep."

The side of the mountain around Goat Rocks had bulged out. The growth that Swanson saw through the theodolite was apparent to Crandell and Mullineaux who were used to seeing a different slope. Now, a giant bulge grew as rock was pushed farther and farther away from the mountain.

The scientists who had come in from California and Hawaii

weren't as familiar with the mountain as Crandell and Mullineaux; they didn't realize with their naked eyes how dramatically Mount St. Helens had changed.

So appallingly sheer, Mullineaux thought immediately. *No one should be up here.*

Mullineaux stopped walking and just stared. "The bulge was terrifying," he said. "I wanted to turn around and leave."

Crandell and Mullineaux swallowed their fear and stayed, barely able to tear their eyes away from the bulge. Swanson explained his measurements to them, and, while they discussed the data, he peered through the theodolite once more.

"Strange," he told the other two, his voice betraying a hint of excitement, as he began to think through the numbers as he wrote them down. "I'd set the crosshairs [of the instrument] on a rock point. Two minutes ago it seemed a bit higher, now a bit lower—like it's moving up and down."

That couldn't be right . . . could it? Swanson brushed off the movement as the sun playing tricks on the instruments. No one had ever heard of the earth quivering like that.

CHAPTER 9

UP, OUT, OR DOWN?

CRANDELL HAD ALREADY CALLED BARRY VOIGHT. THEY NEEDED to learn about landslides.

Voight had come from a famous family—his father had been a professional golfer, and his two younger brothers were an actor (Jon, who was also the father of actress Angelina Jolie) and a songwriter (Chip Taylor, who wrote "Angel of the Morning" and "Wild Thing"). But Barry, the eldest Voight brother, had been more interested in science than celebrity. He was a civil engineer and a geologist, with a special interest in landslides.

Voight arrived at Mount St. Helens on Friday, April 11. Though he was an expert at sudden changes of dirt, rock, snow, and ice, being on an active volcano was a new experience for him. As Voight and Richard Waitt, a USGS volcanologist who was his guide, jotted notes at Timberline, their car started to shudder.

"Tall firs lurched, bushes swayed, rocks tumbled to the snow. Waves rolled down the road like swells on a sea. We wobbled north-south, north-south for five seconds," Waitt remembered.

Voight looked over, puzzled.

"Earthquake!" Waitt explained.

Voight was a long way from home.

They stopped in to see Harry Truman, who was always willing to tell anyone his opinion of the mountain. ("You don't so much converse with Harry Truman as listen, amused, to a raspy monologue," Waitt remembered.)

"I've been here fifty-four years," Truman affirmed once again. "This is my life. It scares me sometimes now, but I couldn't leave this place." He gestured across Spirit Lake. "I've a cave stocked with food, whiskey, cat food, Christmas lights . . . If anything big happens I'll go across, ride out any trouble . . . I've lived life clean as an angel's drawers."

The two scientists eventually said goodbye and kept moving. Truman might think he could endure whatever was coming, but Voight was determined to find out for sure.

Voight spent the night at the Coldwater observation post. There wasn't much, just a clearing of snow against rocks and trees, so he pitched a tent. For two days he camped out, watched, and made notes.

During the night, earthquakes shook the land as Voight tried to sleep. In the morning, he looked out toward the volcano once more.

Cracks that had been familiar the day before seemed like they'd widened overnight. And a new graben—the seismologists used the German word meaning "ditch"—had formed. For something like that to appear overnight, the ground around the mountain must have moved hundreds of yards.

Must have moved . . . or be moving.

When Voight came down from Coldwater, he drove straight

to the USGS offices in Vancouver. Dirty from camping, with his rubber boots covered in mud and his wool shirt smelling like campfire, Voight pulled Crandell aside. His conclusion was dramatic.

"A slide could be gigantic," Voight told Crandell. And that wasn't even the worst part. "When that much rock goes, the pressure drop on magma below would be huge . . . *That* could trigger eruption."

First the earth would fall away in a massive landslide down the mountain, and then hot gases, lava, and rock could erupt from the newly empty space.

"*That* eruption gives no warning," Crandell replied, shocked.

"No," Voight responded in agreement.

At the press conference that followed, Crandell's voice and words took a new turn. Calmly, as always, he began to tell the assembled reporters and law enforcement officers what Voight had just told him.

"Massive landslide could remove half [of the northern slope], maybe trigger large eruption," one volcanologist remembered hearing. "The slide could sweep down to Spirit Lake, dam it to a high level. Mudflows would sluice down valley . . . the whole cracked north flank could slide."

The words might have been calmly said, but there was no concealing the violence of what had been uttered.

"In our many meetings," the county sheriff said, "Mullineaux and Crandell have been so guarded—maybe this, maybe not. Perhaps big, probably not. Only now have we an idea how bad it could be. The whole Spirit Lake basin, all the lodges and cabins, could be destroyed. Why didn't they say so? We've squandered weeks in preparation."

But Crandell, Mullineaux, and the others had been honest. They turned over their analysis as soon as they had it. There was good reason to try to keep calm, and they knew the limits of their science. The data they had could only lead them so far into the future and no more. They refused, as good scientists should, to overstate what they knew.

On the other hand, David Johnston had been concerned about a violent eruption since the moment he set foot on Mount St. Helens. Even before Barry Voight's visit, Johnston had worried about the story of one unusual volcano in particular.

In September 1955, Mount Bezymianny had begun to shake with earthquakes, just as Mount St. Helens had. Three weeks later, it had erupted. Violently. Devastation stretched for an incredible twenty miles around the mountain.

Johnston and the others were used to hearing about volcanoes exploding. Yet what made Mount Bezymianny remarkable was that instead of exploding *up* toward the sky, it had erupted *out*.

In a scene that sounded remarkably like what Voight had just told Crandell, the force of the eruption was directed laterally, out from the side of the volcano. Everything in front of the blast had been destroyed.

But Mount Bezymianny was behind the iron curtain of communism, a thousand miles northeast of Japan, buried in a remote section of the Union of Soviet Socialist Republics (USSR), which is now Russia. It was hard to trust the stories and half-told tales that seemed more like rumor than fact.

A volcano erupting sideways? Could that really happen at Mount St. Helens?

Voight seemed to think yes. Johnston was worried, too.

And if Mount St. Helens erupted out the side, the destruction, like the destruction around Mount Bezymianny, would be horrific.

There was just one problem.

Right as everyone began to agree on the danger, the mountain seemed to go back to sleep.

CHAPTER 10

QUIET

Excuse us, mountain

Mount St. Helens' celebrity is beginning to wane. The once-in-a-lifetime experience [for] geologists has become a bureaucratic problem how to pay for [it] . . . None of us can afford . . . attention to the tantrum. Thanks for the show, St. Helens. [But] we've other business to attend to . . . Do keep in touch.
—*THE COLUMBIAN*

THE HARMONIC TREMORS, WHICH ROLLED THE GROUND FOR AS long as thirty minutes at a time, had stopped on April 12. Large earthquakes, which had been coming at the rate of one an hour in late March, went down to one per day by April 11. Then, as if to seal the conclusion that the mountain was winding back down, the steam-blast eruptions—the "burps" of gas and ash—ended on April 22.

Just as everyone was finally—finally!—agreeing that the mountain was dangerous, it seemed to retreat to safety.

Yes, some earthquakes continued. Yes, these earthquakes were rather large. But they weren't the harmonic tremors that signaled the movement of magma.

And yes, some of the cracks in the mountain's crater were still issuing gas. And yes, the scientists couldn't get down to these vents to sample them (and find out what the gas might be able to tell them) because ice avalanches were dangerous inside the crater. But it was all a lot less dramatic than the blasting eruptions of the past month or so.

And yes, the bulge was still growing. But by this point, even that was a bit of old news. The growth was so constant, so steady. It rose at almost exactly six and a half feet per day—every day— away from the mountain. It was just so predictable. Barry Voight had left, returning to Pennsylvania State University to write up his findings on a possible landslide. And after all, it was just a *possible* landslide, right?

Even the scientists at the USGS offices in Vancouver, Washington, couldn't seem to quite muster the anxiety they felt a month ago.

There is "no indication [of] major eruption . . . in the near future," read the official statement from the USGS.

It was a far cry from the press conference where Barry Voight had announced his prediction.

Yet the words of one scientist, over a *possible* landslide and eruption, were hard to reconcile with the evidence the mountain was providing firsthand.

It seemed like Mount St. Helens had quieted down.

CHAPTER 11

KEEP THEM AWAY

WHEN LAW ENFORCEMENT OFFICERS ASKED FOR MORE ROAD-blocks and more officers to enforce the blocks, their director denied their request.

"No, it'd waste our time. The mountain's going back to sleep," said the director.

Still, the officers on the ground did what they could and tried to keep people away, even though it was pointless to try to block the roads. Only the land above the tree line had been officially closed by the state government. The officers couldn't really enforce a block without authorization. Plus, they were all too aware of the double standard being laid down between the loggers and the tourists.

"One day I stop by the [road] block," Washington State Patrol Captain Dick Bullock recalled. "I'm telling sightseers they can't pass because it's dangerous. But now *down* the highway comes a Weyerhaeuser truck with a load of logs. 'If it's really dangerous,' says the tourist, 'why're they up there? If it's safe for them, why isn't it safe for us?' I've no good answer to this."

But the mountain had gone quiet. Or, at least, quieter. And trying to keep people from their jobs, from the livelihoods that put food on their plate and a roof over their heads, was as dangerous as the mountain next door.

"Many loggers can't work winters when the woods are full of snow," explained Bullock. "They can't now [in spring] take a day off. Work puts food on the family table . . . We officers block people from jobs because something might happen. *Might.* Facing them at a roadgate, you can't but empathize."

Eventually, they reached a compromise—Weyerhaeuser, law enforcement, the Forest Service, and the USGS scientists. They would close the mountain and the area around it in two sections: a Blue Zone extending farthest away that would be closed to tourists but open to loggers, and a Red Zone closest to the danger, open only to those scientists monitoring the volcano, law enforcement, emergency teams if needed . . . and Harry Truman.

Governor Dixy Lee Ray didn't approve of the two-phase plan. "Well, the idea of a Blue Zone is stupid," the outspoken governor said. "It's either dangerous or not."

But the agreement would finally close the state land, rather than just blocking the road. And it would let the loggers keep their jobs in the Blue Zone. Governor Ray signed Executive Order 80–05 into law. For the first time since the mountain had started shaking and erupting, land below the timberline was closed.

It didn't come a moment too soon.

The mountain's short nap was done.

CHAPTER 12

VERIFY

BY THE SECOND WEEK IN MAY, MOUNT ST. HELENS HAD returned in full force. The crater began puffing ash once more. The harmonic tremors rolled once again.

Mindy Brugman had spent the past month far from the reach of the volcano. She and a group of friends had gone backcountry mountain climbing and skiing, crossing over glaciers and racing down snowy peaks hundreds of miles away from Mount St. Helens. But when she came back to the California Institute of Technology in early May and heard what was happening at Mount St. Helens, she knew she had to get up to the volcano.

Brugman was a glaciologist, a scientist who studied the movement of glaciers. She had spent months in the summer and again in the winter examining and taking data on the Shoestring Glacier, which wound its way down from the top of Mount St. Helens. She had even been up on the mountain in February, less than a month before it began to erupt. She knew it well.

In May, when she finally reached the mountain, she found that the water in the glacier's cracks was "really hot! Like really warm, warm enough for a hot tub," she later remembered.

It was another sign that magma was heating the glacier from below.

By this point, the bulge's dramatic change of the mountain's surface was easy to see with the naked eye. But the instruments they were using to measure growth were clunky and took a lot of time and energy to analyze. Within days of her arrival at Mount St. Helens, Brugman realized that a much faster instrument—a ruby laser ranger—would help speed up the process and give a confirmation to the numbers that they already had. She had used one the previous summer to measure the movement of the Shoestring Glacier; she was sure it would help now.

So she went up to the USGS glaciology offices in Tacoma, and she asked for permission to use the instrument.

"It's sitting on your shelf, and I know how to use it. Can I bring it down?" Mindy asked her old boss, Steve Hodge.

"No," Hodge replied. "Because if the mountain blows up, it's going to wreck our instrument."

If the mountain blew up, it was going to do a lot more than just wreck instruments.

With lives hanging in the balance, Brugman pressed further. She went over Hodge's head and set up a meeting with his boss, Mark Meier. She knew that more accurate, faster measurements were needed to verify the movement the USGS scientists were seeing at the bulge.

She made her case to Meier. At the end of their conversation, Meier agreed that she should take the instrument. But the ruby laser ranger wasn't his to give out.

"Well, you need to ask Steve," Meier said.

Brugman hung her head. "Yeah. I already have," she admitted. And she repeated Hodge's reasoning.

Meier pounded his fist on the table between them. "That's the stupidest thing I've ever heard! You go get that instrument and you take it down there and you help them, and you take any of my employees that you want to go with you!"

And she did.

Brugman came back to Mount St. Helens bearing the ruby laser ranger. She added nine more measurement points to the bulge.

Accurate down to the centimeter, the new instrument confirmed what the other measurements had said: day and night, the bulge steadily grew.

Some scientists believed, or hoped, that the bulge was swelling with water melted from the glaciers. But Brugman had already studied the glacier melt on Mount St. Helens. She knew that water would never cause the mountain to grow like that.

There was only one thing that could force such swelling: molten-hot magma.

CHAPTER 13

THE TOUTLE RIVER

CRANDELL HAD CONVINCED THE RESIDENTS AND BUSINESS owners of Spirit Lake to leave the area. (All but Harry Truman, and he seemed unmovable. So long as there was a camera or a reporter nearby, he wouldn't go anywhere. "After all the press talk he thinks he'll look silly if he goes out and nothing happens. He's painted into a corner. He's only human," one sheriff said about Truman.)

But the residents of Spirit Lake weren't the only ones living by Mount St. Helens.

Rumors were spreading rapidly up and down the Toutle River. People who lived in Castle Rock, Kid Valley, Silver Lake, and Toutle were worried. Neighbor had whispered to neighbor that a hundred-foot wall of water could come crashing down the river. Someone else had heard that a landslide could send all the water in Spirit Lake down into the valley.

They asked Mullineaux to come and tell them directly: What danger were they in?

One hundred and thirty people gathered in Toutle Lake High School on Friday, May 9, to hear him speak.

"The river should flood no more than in the last two eruptions," Mullineaux said, as he drew diagrams and explained the evidence they had found from the past. Many of their fears were unfounded. A landslide would dam Spirit Lake and hold water in, not create a surge out.

However, he told them to prepare to evacuate to high ground if the mountain did erupt. The water in Spirit Lake would stay put, but glacier melt and groundwater released from an eruption could create a fast-moving lahar.

"Mud could reach houses less than twenty feet above the river," he said. "Be ready to leave."

It was a meeting typical of what everyone had come to expect from Mullineaux—warnings of danger cushioned in a peaceful voice, wild fears and rumors tempered by the limits of past eruptions.

GEOLOGIST CALMS TOUTLE, the *Daily News* reported the next day. Which wasn't, perhaps, the only conclusion Mullineaux would've wanted the people to take from his talk. Even Donna duBeth, though, could only at best write GEOLOGISTS AT ODDS ON ERUPTION CHANCES.

"Trying to pin down a geologist [is] like trying to corner a rat in a rain barrel," Cowlitz County Sheriff Les Nelson muttered to a reporter. For rescue workers and law enforcement, it might have been easier if the people were just a bit scared.

In their defense, Mullineaux and Crandell believed in the balance they struck between caution and living. They trusted their assessment of risk so much that they moved the scientists' outpost even closer to the mountain. The station they had established above Coldwater Creek seemed too far away to provide a timely warning of eruption. So they moved nearer.

In early May, snow still covered the high ridges around Mount St. Helens. Weyerhaeuser bulldozers were called to clear old logging roads once more. The scientists set up on a clearing just five and a half miles from the volcano, which gave them an unobstructed, closer view of the mountaintop.

A graduate student named Harry Glicken, who worked for David Johnston, came to live at the site, which they named Coldwater II (and began referring to the original Coldwater site as Coldwater I).

One of Crandell's colleagues had studied the area; the only signs of eruptions over the past thousand years at Coldwater II were marks of hot ash. It wasn't ideal, but a bit of hot ash was survivable. They saw no evidence of magma, lahars, or pyroclastic flows. It should be safe; after all, five and a half miles seemed far from the volcano.

Glicken's mission at Coldwater II? To watch the bulge.

It kept growing. It never stopped.

Barry Voight was still thinking about the bulge, too. Back in Pennsylvania, he had written a report predicting a giant landslide. But more than that, he also wrote about what the change from a landslide could do to fluid underneath the ground. If the bulge were to slip away, it would be like the top was taken off a shaken-up bottle of champagne. All that pressure inside would suddenly be released.

The landslide would be catastrophic. The explosion afterward would be worse.

Voight dated his report May 1, 1980. But it wouldn't be read in Vancouver for almost three weeks. By then, it would be too late.

CHAPTER 14

A Scouting Problem

Spirit Lake was over two miles long. While the Indigenous people had avoided the area and called it Tesemini, or Lake of Spirits, European settlers enjoyed the cold, clear water. For more than a century, people had come to swim and camp under the firs that towered hundreds of feet overhead. What had begun as a simple wagon road had been paved over and widened as campgrounds and resorts had sprung up along its path until more than a thousand people spent each weekend by the shores of the lake.

By the beginning of May, they were all gone. (Except, of course, Harry Truman.) But leaving is never easy. Resort managers had left property and animals that needed care. Residents knew that people had been trespassing into the Red Zone, and they were worried about vandalism.

The YMCA and the Boy Scouts each had camps around the lake. Both had decided to close for the summer, but if they were going to be able to continue summer plans elsewhere, then they needed the gear that was stored at Spirit Lake.

When he heard their plight, Governor Ray's press secretary, Ray Walters, took pity on the two programs. He wrote an exception note to the Red Zone executive order, allowing them legal passage to Spirit Lake.

Of course, word got out.

Now everyone knew that the governor or her people were willing to make exceptions. If they let in the Boy Scouts, then everyone else who owned property and equipment around the lake wanted to retrieve their belongings, too. But without any high-ranking connections, they didn't have a way to ask for an exemption to the Red Zone executive order.

The residents decided to take matters into their own hands: They would gather together and run the roadblock on Saturday morning.

By Friday, May 16, rumors of the convoy had reached the governor.

State Patrol Chief Robert Landon spoke up. He told her that he had okay'ed the exemption earlier in the week after approval had come down from her office. It came as a complete surprise to Governor Ray. She was furious.

"As a [Boy Scouts] Scoutmaster, you've a soft spot for them," she roared at her press secretary when she found out what Walters had done. "Now we've little choice but to let people in."

She had signed the executive order to keep people away; now she was forced to let a caravan through. Washington State Police began coordinating with the Skamania County sheriff. Neither set of officers wanted to get anywhere close to the mountain, but it would be better to escort people peacefully than face an angry mob.

Even before the caravan had been arranged or the Boy Scouts and YMCA had been let in, however, another plan was already being drafted to keep people safe. The state patrol, the county sheriffs, Washington's Department of Emergency Services, and Weyerhaeuser were working once again with the scientists in Vancouver to come up with a new map of the area around the mountain. Together, they decided to extend both the Blue Zone and Red Zone.

The plan was completed on Friday, May 16. It reached Governor Ray's office that afternoon.

But she had already left. She wouldn't be back in the office—she wouldn't see the new plan—until after the weekend. It would have to wait until Monday.

The convoy to Spirit Lake, however, was still on for Saturday morning.

Several reporters decided to join the residents. But in her month and a half of covering the mountain's eruption, Donna duBeth had seen enough.

"You want to go tomorrow?" her colleague asked her on Friday night.

"No. The mountain's a monster," she replied.

"Metaphors like that exaggerate. No one knows what'll happen."

"It'll be *terrible*."

She had reported on Mount St. Helens for long enough to have listened to the scientists, to have witnessed the bulge growing and the mountain shaking and erupting.

DuBeth drove home to Seattle and didn't look back.

Harry Glicken couldn't stay at Coldwater II. He had been there for weeks, watching, documenting, and making notes, but he had a job interview in California. Friday would have to be his last night. Don Swanson volunteered to take his spot starting on Sunday.

There was one night missing. Someone had to be at the research post on Saturday night, between when Glicken left and Swanson arrived.

David Johnston volunteered.

That night, he called his girlfriend in California.

"I think it's near eruption," he said. "It scares me."

More than once, though, he had told her, "If I die young, I hope it's in an eruption."

※

Very, very early on Friday morning, May 16—just before dawn—a plane made nine passes over Mount St. Helens. Flying covertly for the Department of Energy, the plane carried some of the most technologically advanced infrared cameras. It could detect the heat from a cup of coffee from over five thousand feet—nearly a mile—away!

Later that day, the plane returned to its hanger, and the film was set aside. The images from the infrared camera were expensive to process and analyze, and the USGS was already far over budget. There wasn't money to pay another person to work overtime on the weekend.

If the film had been developed and examined that weekend, the scientists would have realized that there was enough heat energy coming from the mountain to power a thousand homes.

More concerningly, they would've seen that new spots of heat were coming almost exclusively from around the bulge.

But working on the weekend cost money.

The film would wait until Monday.

SATURDAY, MAY 17, 1980

CHAPTER 15

CONVOY

ONE VAN PAINTED WITH "DIXY OPEN THE GATE" SEEMED TO speak for everyone in the caravan. Cars snaked down Spirit Lake Highway, residents and property owners, waiting to legally enter the Red Zone.

"It's dangerous, like playing Russian roulette with the volcano," grumbled Skamania Sheriff Bill Closner.

But the sheriff had his orders.

When the convoy reached Spirit Lake, the residents dispersed to their homes. The reporters, however, went to see Harry Truman.

"Everybody in the [explative deleted] country's up here!" Truman growled at them.

But his anger was a façade, easily seen through after a few minutes of talking. He was scared, though he refused every offer of a car or helicopter ride down the mountain and out to safety.

When it came time for everyone to leave, his eyes welled up as he gripped one of the trooper's arms. When the trooper, too, began to get teary, Truman fell back on his strongman act of bravado.

"Oh, c'mon," Truman whispered, "let's keep a stiff upper lip."

By 7:45 p.m., all thirty-five people who had signed waivers to enter the Red Zone had signed back out.

CHAPTER 16

AT COLDWATER II

"THE BULGE LOOKED *HUGE*, INFLATED LIKE A BALLOON," REMEM-bered Mindy Brugman, who came to Coldwater II with another scientist, Carolyn Driedger, on Saturday to train David Johnston on the ruby laser ranger. Johnston was taking over for Harry Glicken, and he needed to know how to use the new instrument.

The four scientists and friends spent a beautiful day watching the mountain. They talked and laughed, enjoying the view and the spring afternoon. As day began to turn to dusk, Brugman and Driedger went to their car and began pulling out sleeping bags.

As soon as they did, Johnston's entire demeanor changed. Immediately, he began to tell them to put their camping gear back.

"This place may be dangerous!" he said. "A landslide off the bulge could uncork a hot flow across the valley and up this ridge."

"You'll be fine," Brugman insisted.

"No," Johnston countered. "The blast could go down, the landslides could go down. And the blast could come up right over here . . . No, you're not safe here."

"That's hard to believe," said Brugman.

"Oh yes," Johnston assured her, "it could . . . [it's] too risky.

Only one's needed here. Let's have as few people as possible," he said, firmly.

"Reluctantly," remembered Driedger, "we put our gear back."

Brugman and Driedger drove to their rooms in Vancouver, promising to come back the next day. Glicken stayed a while longer, but he left eventually, too.

Johnston was alone at Coldwater II.

CHAPTER 17

On a Desk

On a desk in Vancouver, Barry Voight's report predicting a landslide followed by an enormous eruption sat, unread.

On a desk in Olympia, the new, expanded plan to keep everyone farther away from the mountain sat, unsigned.

On a desk in Las Vegas, film from infrared cameras revealing new, dangerous sources of heat coming from the bulge sat, unopened and unexamined.

They would all be too late to help.

CHAPTER 18

THE MOUNTAIN

FOR ALMOST TWO MONTHS, MOUNT ST. HELENS HAD BEEN SHAK-
ing, erupting, and swelling.

The crater had grown to 1,300 feet in diameter. Two giant
arrays of cracks spread across the entire summit area.

The bulge on the north side of the mountain was—and had
been for over a month—expanding at six and a half feet every day.
By May 18, the top reached 140 meters (almost 450 feet) above the
ground. The surface of the bulge continued to crack and break,
distorting from pressure underneath.

More than 10,000 earthquakes had shaken the mountain
since mid-March. Though harmonic tremors had ceased again
after May 8, twenty to forty earthquakes still shook the ground
every day. Two large earthquakes were recorded on May 8 and 12.

The eruptions had stopped.

Gas issued from small vents called fumaroles, but the plumes
of ash and steam and gas had ended on May 14.

On the night of May 17, many people driving along roads saw
animals skitter out and wildly dart back into the forest.

The animals were afraid.

MAY 18, 1980—8:32 A.M.

CHAPTER 19

ZERO MILES: 1,000 FEET ABOVE THE MOUNTAIN

THE PLANE RIDE WAS A BIRTHDAY PRESENT. KEITH STOFFEL HAD chartered it for his wife, Dorothy, taking advantage of the fact that they were visiting Yakima, close to Mount St. Helens. Tourists weren't allowed in the airspace around the mountain, but Dorothy and Keith were both geologists; they knew the right people to talk to for permission. Early in the morning on May 18, 1980, officials at the USGS offices in Vancouver gave their flight the go-ahead to circle the summit and take pictures.

They reached Mount St. Helens before 8:00 a.m. Pilot Bruce Judson circled three times, bringing them down to only five hundred feet above the crater.

"What amazed me," Dorothy later remembered, "was how serene it was."

It was a gorgeous day. The clouds that so often blocked the summit from view were nowhere in sight. The sun shone brightly.

But all was not—exactly—as it should have been.

"On the north side," Dorothy recalled, "we could see water from melting snow and ice. It was as though the mountain was weeping." Even the surface of the mountain was showing signs of the tremendous heat coming from within.

They flew around the mountain for forty minutes, talking and taking pictures, discussing the ash-streaked snow. Just after 8:30 a.m., they began their final pass. They flew clockwise, coming from the south, rising to a thousand feet above the summit.

They drew closer. Dorothy clicked away, capturing images of the stalwart Shoestring Glacier sitting astride the mountain's rocky top.

Then the ice of the glacier fell into the crater.

It was 8:32 a.m.

East to west, a crack tore the mountain apart. Then the rock itself began to "vibrate," said Keith.

"The whole north side of the mountain became almost fluid," said Dorothy, "like someone was slicing the mountain in half."

"Huge east-west waves undulated like agitated jello," said Keith. It was "eerie . . . The entire mass began to ripple and churn up, without moving laterally."

Then in the next moments, the ground was moving, flowing.

The bulge was gone, hurtling down the mountainside, gathering speed and power and debris as it went.

Barry Voight was right—the bulge had just detached as the largest landslide ever recorded.

Barry Voight was *right*—seconds later, the eruption began.

There was almost no time at all, a blink of the eye, a heartbeat or two, before a frothing mass of black and dark, dark gray exploded from the empty space.

Oh dear, this is the big one and here we are right above it, thought Dorothy.

Bruce stayed calm. He dipped the plane's wings and told the Stoffels to take pictures.

"I slid across the back seat," said Keith. "A thousand feet below the airplane the mile-wide face of the mountain was flowing, picking up speed. Below us, a huge explosion, but I felt and heard nothing. Its gray and frothy cloud billowed beneath us and plunged north [down the mountain]. Within seconds it blocked my view of Spirit Lake."

The clouds from the landslide and lateral blast were moving down and away. But from the summit, another raging mass began erupting up. And spreading out.

It was coming right for them.

"We gotta get out of here!" Keith screamed.

A frothing plume of ash and gas and rock and ice rose toward them. "The cloud swelled fast, chasing us. In a few more seconds it grew to a mile and more," Keith said.

Dorothy turned around, looking behind her to the summit. She swore.

Bruce dove. He pitched the nose of the airplane down, pushing past the red "never exceed" line on the air speed indicator of his Cessna 182. They were flying at 205 miles per hour.

"Go faster!" Dorothy yelled, pounding on the front panel of the plane.

Bruce pushed the plane's nose down even more. They were past redline now, flying at 220 miles per hour and in danger of ripping the plane's wings off.

But the blast was moving hundreds of miles an hour—they would never outrun it.

I'm going to disappear, thought Dorothy, convinced she was about to die. *[My Mother's] not going to know what happened to me.*

"Turn right!" Keith yelled.

They couldn't outrun it, but perhaps they could hide. The southern side of the volcano—on the opposite side of the mountain from the bulge—was relatively calm.

"The trees grew larger and larger," Dorothy said as they dove and Bruce swung the plane behind the mountain.

When they looked to the summit, massive clouds were rising in the air. "It was billowing up, almost like in big pillow-sort-of structures," said Dorothy. But there was nothing comforting about its appearance.

Tremendous lightning flashed within the cloud. Thousands and thousands of lightning bolts. So much that "we could actually see into the crater," said Dorothy. The cavernous walls were illuminated like daylight.

The landslide had come crashing away from the mountain, the lateral blast had exploded out the side, and a dark column was spewing tens of thousands of feet into the air. But Dorothy, Keith, and Bruce heard nothing but the thrum of their plane's propeller. To them, the eruption was silent.

"We neither felt nor heard a thing," Keith said.

Through the silence, the trees grew larger as Bruce dove to the south. His bet worked. The eruption didn't hunt them there. He finally leveled off just above the forest and slowed the plane to 180 miles an hour.

Nothing was chasing them. Nothing reached them on the south side.

They had escaped an erupting volcano.

They were shaking as their plane landed at Portland International Airport. The moment the plane stopped moving, all three of them jumped out and ran.

"I began to recognize that Keith and Bruce were running with me . . . We were all nonverbal, just running," said Dorothy.

They fled, sprinting from the plane that had witnessed their terror.

"We got to the terminal, and then we realized we'd left my purse and our cameras on the plane. We looked out on the tarmac, and there was our little plane with the doors wide open," said Dorothy.

They had come running in, without any thought to securing the plane or their possessions.

More than forty years later, Dorothy would laugh as she recounted the moment. The joy, the disbelief, the shock of having lived and having outrun a volcano was still present as if it had been only yesterday.

Their first thought after realizing they were safe, even before they had landed in Portland, was to let others know of the danger. While they were still in the air, Bruce had called over the radio to Seattle Center air traffic control.

"The whole north side of the mountain went! It's erupting!" he exclaimed.

"What level?" they asked.

"The whole mountain!"

"Well, how large is it?"

He swore and screamed, "*big!*"

But the air traffic controllers only rolled their eyes. "Here's *another* [pilot] telling us the mountain's erupted," one said to another.

They were used to getting reports about Mount St. Helens erupting—it had been erupting for a month and a half already.

They didn't realize that *this* was the eruption everyone had been dreading.

CHAPTER 20

COLDWATER II: 5 AND A HALF MILES FROM THE MOUNTAIN

THE STOFFELS HAD FLOWN SOUTH BECAUSE THE LANDSLIDES AND lateral blast had come from the bulge on the north.

Coldwater II was directly in its path.

The ridge was 1,300 feet above the river, five and a half miles from the summit.

It wasn't far enough.

Johnston had been watching the mountain. He saw the bulge slide away. He saw the blast coming after.

"Vancouver! Vancouver!" he cried over the radio, his voice excited and not fearful. "This is it!"

Scientists as far away as Seattle heard his words.

Moments later, David Johnston died in the eruption of Mount St. Helens.

CHAPTER 21

Spirit Lake

The bulge slid away, and the blast following it overtook the avalanche within seconds. Moving at 350 miles per hour, the super-heated cloud of gas and ash reached Spirit Lake at almost the same moment it did David Johnston at Coldwater II.

No one heard Harry Truman's last words before he was swept away.

CHAPTER 22

8 Miles North

GERRY MARTIN WAS AN AMATEUR SCIENTIST. HE HAD SAID HE was "spotting for the state" as part of the Radio Amateur Civil Emergency Services group. From a clearing on a ridge, above forks of Coldwater Creek, he had a view of Mount St. Helens.

Gerry, like Johnston, saw what was coming.

"Earthquake . . . shakin'," Gerry reported over his ham radio at 8:32 a.m.

Twenty-seven seconds later, he came back on the radio: "Now we've got an eruption down here . . . a big slide coming off . . . Now we got a whole great big eruption out of the crater. And . . . another one opened up on the west side. The whole . . . north side is slidin' down."

"Keep goin', Gerry," another ham radio operator added, when Martin paused his description.

"All right," Gerry replied. "The whole . . . north section blowing up, trying to."

He watched as the frothing cloud engulfed Coldwater II. "Camper and car sittin' over to the south of me is covered," he reported, as he saw the eruption take David Johnston.

Then he added: "It's gonna get me too."

Martin's last transmission came two minutes and four seconds after he first reported an earthquake.

✳

Other operators, other "spotting" volunteers farther away, kept talking over the radio after Martin went silent. The coordinator in Olympia, Washington asked for more details and relayed their reports to the state Emergency Management Division.

". . . you wouldn't believe it," one spotter said. "It's covering an area 15 or 20 miles in length and it's going clean up in the clouds now. It's . . . black . . . it's unbelievable . . . It keeps boiling . . . at the bottom, boiling and boiling."

"You did say it was blowing north?" the coordinator in Olympia asked.

"It's going . . . northeast," a second operator chimed in.

"The cloud went northwest," a third contradicted.

"Well, it's going all directions now," came the second operator's reply.

CHAPTER 23

11 Miles Northwest

BARRY WAS HUNGRY.

Bea and Barry Johnston had gotten up early that morning and driven toward Spud Mountain, a mere seven miles from Mount St. Helens. Their friend Jim Fitzgerald had agreed to meet them there, and he was probably already on-site, getting awesome sunrise pictures. The weather was *perfect*—they were going to get some truly fantastic shots.

But Barry was hungry.

"Y'know I don't want to sit up there all day without breakfast," he whined.

"You never want breakfast!" Bea replied.

"I do now."

They had driven almost all the way to the mountain, but they turned around.

It was an uncomfortable breakfast at Toutle Café. Bea was furious they were missing the sunrise and all the great pictures that Jim was getting. She didn't bother to hide that she was mad.

But finally—*finally*—full of toast and eggs, they got back on Spirit Lake Highway once more, headed toward Jim and Spud Mountain.

From the road, all they could see were tall fir trees; the forest blocked Mount St. Helens from view.

Then they came around a bend. They should've had a clear view. The mountain should have been looming above.

It wasn't there.

"A convoluting gray cloud had piled where Mount St. Helens should be," said Bea.

Barry, who was driving, pulled over. He and Bea leaped from the car and began taking pictures.

I missed it! Bea thought, realizing that the mountain had erupted. *On the ridge, Jim's getting great shots. I'm not because of breakfast!*

The cloud grew bigger. "Much lightning flashed in it," Bea remembered.

But just like the Stoffels had noticed from the air, Bea was amazed that "the show was silent. No noise with something so big; the brain can't comprehend what's happening."

Bea thought that she was going into shock.

She took more pictures as the cloud rolled over Elk Rock in the distance. The ridge did nothing to stop the rush of oncoming destruction. She watched as the cloud came up and over the crest, crashing down the opposite side.

It was headed right toward them.

"We've got to get out of here!" Bea yelled.

"Yeah," Barry agreed. "Let's move!"

They jumped back into their Jeep and peeled away, turning in a wide arc across the road. Their speedometer topped out at eighty miles an hour, and with his foot to the floor, Barry had them at the limit.

The cloud was gaining on them.

"Ohmygod!" Bea cried. "Close the windows! We're gonna die!"

"I can't go faster!" Barry yelled. He was already taking curves on two wheels.

Bea was terrified, but she crawled into the back to take more pictures. The cloud was coming so fast, so full of lightning; it was much too big to get in one frame of her camera.

It almost seemed like they were outrunning it when Barry sped around a corner and screeched to a stop.

A motorhome was trying to turn around. It had blocked the whole road.

"The cloud seemed to start up," Bea remembered, as she watched it race toward them, seeming to gain speed.

They couldn't move. The motorhome filled the road. Trees pressed on either side. The cloud—the lightning, the blackness—was coming faster and faster.

There was nothing they could do except sit, helpless.

Finally, the tiniest sliver of road appeared next to the motorhome. Barry punched the gas pedal.

They kept driving and speeding on. Behind them, the cloud seemed to grow just a bit smaller. Then a little bit more. Many miles later, they put real, permanent distance between them and the eruption.

They stopped when they reached high ground. Bea took more

pictures as the cloud began to rise, lifting off from where it had chased them on the ground.

"The cloud was swelling into a mushroom, looking like an atom bomb had gone off," Barry remembered.

They had made it. They were, unbelievably, safe.

"Except for Barry's breakfast," Bea remembered ruefully, "we'd be up *in* that stuff."

For now, there was nothing to do but watch the cloud and wonder whether their friend Jim had survived, too.

✸

At 8:32 a.m., Jim Fitzgerald was already at Spud Mountain. He had arrived before his friends Bea and Barry Johnston. He had come to take pictures of the smoldering volcano, and his camera was out and ready.

His first pictures came as the ash cloud and landslides shot away to the north. Then, as the cloud began to move west as well as north, he took still more pictures. Only after his thirteenth shot did he finally rip the camera from its tripod, run for his car, take one more picture on the fly, and stuff the camera bag under his seat.

The blast overtook him moments later.

CHAPTER 24

11 MILES NORTH

THE SMELL OF PANCAKES AND EGGS WAFTED THROUGH BUZZ Smith's campsite. He had woken up early and started on a big breakfast for his boys, Eric and Adam, who were ten and seven years old. At their camp near the base of a bluff alongside the Green River, Buzz began to fill their backpacks for another day of hiking, trying to lighten their load as much as possible.

"Snow was melting, [there were] many fresh streams, why carry water?" Buzz remembered.

So he dumped the water out of their canteens.

It was a mistake that would haunt him.

The first sign that something was wrong was a few puffs of wind. "That was odd—puffs instead of steady, and reaching us down in big trees," Buzz said.

Crack! Crack! Crack!

"What was that, Dad?" asked Eric.

"Must be someone shooting a rifle back down the river somewhere," answered Buzz, but he knew that wasn't quite right.

"I knelt to fold the tent," Buzz recalled. "I got an uneasy feeling that grew—like an air-pressure change."

Then they looked up.

"A black cloud billowed fast from the south, a thousand feet above the trees. It quickly pulled overhead, and the day grew dim like approaching dusk. It had to be the mountain."

The boys were terrified.

Though Buzz tried to reassure them that it only looked like a little ash, he couldn't help thinking, *actually, it looks like a* lot *of ash*.

Light-gray rocks began falling from the sky. The rocks were hard but not heavy, and when they bounced off the trees and hit Buzz, Eric, and Adam, it didn't hurt.

A few minutes later, the high cloud "pulled back quickly—as if a vacuum sucked it south. The sky above was blue," remembered Buzz.

But Buzz and the boys were far from being safe. The falling rocks were gone, but the real danger was just arriving. The noise and the pressure began to build.

"I felt as though I was being pushed to the ground," Buzz remembered. "A loudening roar came like a low jet. I'd been a Marine and it sounded like an F-4 [fighter jet]. Now I really felt the air being compressed and knew something big was coming."

Ten feet away, a giant cedar tree swayed and crashed to the ground.

"Dad," said Adam, "I've never seen a tree fall down by itself."

Buzz didn't wait. They couldn't outrun what he now realized was the eruption of Mount St. Helens, but there was a way for them to be in the safest place possible.

"When big trees fall," Buzz said, "your best chance is to ride the roots. They hold up the butt end [of the tree] and leave space beneath."

All around them, trees were crashing down.

They needed shelter.

Buzz pulled his sons to huddle at the base of a downed yellow fir that was six feet across. They ripped the sleeping bags out of their packs, zipped them together, and threw the large cover over the trunk. Under the combined sleeping bags, there was a space for the three of them to huddle, crouched together beneath their makeshift roof.

"The ground rumbled and shook—as when you felled a big tree. But there wasn't much noise . . . Ash fell damp and cool like mud. Coarse pellets seemed to come straight down," Buzz remembered.

The ash turned the day to the blackest midnight. Fine particles hung in the air around them, blocking light everywhere. When Buzz took out his flashlight from his pack, it barely illuminated inches in front of him.

Even though the ash was still falling, Buzz decided to see what was happening outside their shelter. He stood up, pushing the sleeping-bag roof aside, and felt through the darkness, stumbling with his hands outstretched in front of him, walking only about ten feet away. He stopped and turned around when he had gone less than the length of a minivan. In air that was completely black, he couldn't even see the ground or footprints where he had just been. He was lost. In a sea of darkness, he realized he couldn't find his way back to the boys.

"Eric!" he shouted. "Adam!"

A faint reply of "Dad! We're here!" barely reached him.

The boys were mere feet away, but the ash muffled the noise so that Buzz almost missed their yells. He followed the thin sound of their voices until he came to their shelter.

"We held each other," Buzz remembered, climbing under the sleeping bag again, and not letting go anymore.

Then the air began to get hot. Really hot. The ground began to shake.

"Rumble and stop. Rumble and stop," Buzz said. "Was the whole mountain exploding? It rumbled ten minutes. Thunder seemed close but muffled, the air too black to see lightning."

When the ground finally stopped shaking, the air seemed to cool a bit as well.

Then they started to get sleepy.

It was warm and dark and silent. Their eyelids felt so heavy . . .

"Daddy," Adam asked, "are we going to live with Jesus?"

"Well, maybe," Buzz said, "but not now!"

Buzz felt a shock race through him that had nothing to do with the eruption. They should *not* be feeling peaceful and content! They needed to be alert! They needed to survive!

"We've got to get *out* of here!" Buzz cried.

Buzz lifted the sleeping bag so that he could stand up. Inches of ash fell to the ground. The soft gray dust was warm, but not hot or burning.

The air had gotten a bit clearer, a bit lighter; Buzz's flashlight could now shine a few feet in front of them. He took a few steps forward.

But when he looked behind him, Buzz still couldn't see his footprints. The ash hanging in the air obscured everything. It was still too dangerous and disorienting to try to make their way out.

They were trapped. There was no choice but to stay where they were, waiting for Mount St. Helens to make its next move.

CHAPTER 25

13 Miles North: Part 1

Six friends had camped in pairs: Sue Ruff with her boyfriend, Bruce Nelson, in one tent, Karen Varner with her boyfriend, Terry Crall, in another, and friends Dan Balch and Brian Thomas in the third, a bit farther away. Sue's dog and Karen's puppies scampered around everyone. They had decided to spend the weekend alongside the Green River. They hadn't seen anyone else on their hike in, but they had parked next to one other car at the trailhead. They didn't know it, but Buzz Smith and his boys were also along the river.

Terry, Sue, and Bruce woke up early that Sunday morning. It was beautiful, peaceful. It would've been relaxing, too, except that Terry caught a fish so big that it snapped the line. His hands were shaking from excitement as he came back to camp. On a Sunday morning, catching—and losing—a really big fish seemed like the most thrilling thing that would happen all day.

Until Terry looked up from winding what was left of the line onto a stick.

"Mygod!" he cried. "There must be a fire!"

Sue, Terry, and Bruce watched as in the distance a "little black cloud grew taller like a rising fire plume," Sue remembered. "But in fifteen seconds it spread not just up but far west . . . and filled a quarter of the sky south of us. It was silent."

"That's no fire!" Terry and Bruce shouted together.

"Suddenly wind roared through the trees from the south," remembered Sue. "Arms of [the cloud] spurted out in front a hundred to a few hundred feet, boiling and branching, the black wall quickly caught up, then other arms shot out . . . the roar of the wind horrendous. With my back to the wind, my hair braids blew straight out in front. I glanced back. The cloud had grown big so fast and was racing straight toward us."

Terry dove into his tent where Karen was still sleeping.

Standing near his own tent, Bruce watched the oncoming cloud, holding a bag of marshmallows, popping them in his mouth one at a time, and backing away slowly.

A couple hundred feet away, the noise had woken Dan Balch and Brian Thomas.

Dan swore, shouting at Brian to get out.

Brian ran from the tent in long underwear, and he dove down into a space two feet high under a fir. Dan, more dressed in jeans, a T-shirt, and socks, barely made it ten feet to the backside of a different fir before the blast hit.

"Within a couple seconds it got darker, then pitch black. The ground vibrated as if many trees came down all at once. The blast knocked me face-down," Dan remembered, "and pushed the air out of me—I couldn't breathe. Mud and ice rained down. I tried to get up, but the air was gone . . . I could see nothing."

On the ground, Dan was breathless and scared, but he wasn't hurt. Brian was not so lucky.

"Trees fell on my big log [shelter] with enough force to roll it," said Brian. "A branch spur caught my right leg and hip, and with great leverage turned me into the ground and out sideways. A sharp pain meant my hip was broken. In darkness I couldn't tell which way was up. I knew this was an eruption. It seemed the end."

A few hundred yards back, Sue had run to Bruce as the cloud enveloped them.

"Sue got to me," Bruce remembered. "I put my arms around her, and everything went black. I heard trees boom down all at once."

"I got thrown onto my back in utter darkness," Sue remembered.

"I smelled fresh dirt," Bruce remembered after he was thrown down, too. *We must be in the hole of an uprooted tree, buried in fallen trees*, he thought.

It was pure luck, and a miracle, that would save them. Down in the dirt, Sue and Bruce were sheltered from the worst that was yet to come.

The temperature was just beginning to rise. Heat had followed the darkness.

"My hair sizzled," remembered Bruce. "I'm a baker who works with huge ovens. This was five or six hundred degrees Fahrenheit."

"It burned the top of my hair," said Sue. "I felt hot pitch boil out of a tree."

"We're dead!" screamed Bruce. "Omygod, we're gonna die, we're gonna die!"

"I was pissed he'd caved in so fast," Sue later remembered.

They cowered underneath the trees, down in the cooler dirt, as hot air blasted all around them.

A few moments later, the intense heat was gone. The air began to cool. They had survived yet another strike from the volcano.

"We're not dead yet!" Sue cried. "Let's try to get out!"

In darkness deeper than midnight, they climbed over the trunks of trees that had protected them. But the bark burned their legs, and the hot ash that blanketed everything around them seared their fingers.

Then, unbelievably, the darkness lifted all at once. They saw blue sky. The air was hazy, but the sun shone.

They could see once more, and every view showed utter devastation.

"Around us was no green, every [pine] needle gone. No sign of our green tent or Terry and Karen's red one," remembered Sue.

Everything they saw had been stripped bare.

But their sight wouldn't last for long.

"Black was coming again—straight down and thick, like a blanket falling," remembered Bruce. "Thick, warm ash fell and we couldn't see again. This time there was no wind. It fell densely, like somebody pouring a bag of fine sand over your head."

"It went totally black again," said Sue.

In the few minutes while they'd been able to see, Sue and Bruce had found their bearings. There was a hill next to them. Instinctively, they headed to higher ground.

They felt their way forward in the absolute darkness. Fallen trees constantly blocked their path, and they pulled themselves up and over on the rough bark. Twice, earthquakes shook the ground. Sue fell off the log she was climbing, and Bruce pulled her back up, their hands managing to find each other in the dark.

The cloud from the eruption pressed against them. Lightning flashed.

"In blackness the lightning weirdly went horizontal. To a loud *crack!* it flashed pinkish and bluish," Sue said.

The air began to reek of sulfur, the rotten-egg smell reminding them of Yellowstone National Park or hot springs around Sue's hometown in Wyoming. They were wearing boots, but even through the thick soles, their feet grew warm from the hot ash. Their mouths went dry from breathing in the ash-filled air, and they pulled their shirts up and over their heads to help filter out what particles they could.

"Some stuff fell wet," remembered Sue. "I felt wet enough on my arms to think it was raining. Larger sharp things stung my arms."

Chunks of ice? Bruce thought. It was confusing in the darkness. Later, they realized that the cloud contained bits of Mount St. Helens's glaciers, which were raining down along with ash, and the ice stung their skin.

They found a stable log and huddled against it, together.

"Sue, if we get out of this, will you marry me?" Bruce asked.

"Yes," Sue answered.

Soon, they both began to feel sleepy. Though the heat had been intense and the ash was still painfully warm to the touch, Sue began to feel cold and nauseous. They tried to keep talking to stay awake.

There was nothing to do but wait and stay together, helping each other fight to stay alive.

*

An hour after the ash began to fall, it seemed like it was perhaps starting to clear. Maybe, just maybe, the darkness was beginning to recede.

"After many more minutes," Bruce said, "we could see ten feet."

Ten feet—not even two body-lengths in front of them. But that was more than they had been able to see before. And just like their instincts to reach higher ground and to fight to stay awake, they knew now that they had to get moving.

Then a noise broke the silence that had followed the blast. They heard something "like a foghorn," Sue said.

The noise came again.

"Karen! Terry!" they shouted. "Brian! Dan!"

There was no response to their cries.

Sue and Bruce worked their way back down toward where the campsite had been. "The beautiful green forest was gone and gray. We were in hell," said Sue.

"Cody! Come on, Cody!" she called to her dog as they came near the tents.

Miraculously, Cody and all of the puppies came out from beneath some trees. Sue cleaned ash from their eyes, but somehow, none of their bones were broken.

The dogs were their only glimmer of hope.

"A big pile of trees lay about where [Karen and Terry's] tent had been," said Bruce. Huge, fallen trunks were strewn across the campsite. Their friends hadn't survived.

Then, just as Sue and Bruce realized what had happened to Karen and Terry, they heard the foghorn-like noise again. This time, they could recognize what it was.

"Hellllp!" called a voice.

Dan was alive.

CHAPTER 26

13 MILES NORTH: PART 2

SUE AND BRUCE RAN AS FAST AS THEY COULD TOWARD THE SOUND of Dan's voice. He was shouting, desperate and hurt. They climbed over downed trees and squeezed between fallen branches, following the sounds of Dan's cries.

Finally, on the opposite side of where they had camped the night before, they found Brian and Dan sitting on a log, together but each severely injured. Brian's hip was broken, and Dan was badly burned—he had weathered the heat of the blast in the open.

While Sue and Bruce had clung to each other in the first moments of the eruption, Dan had stood alone. He had been sheltering behind a tree, but it fell, and there hadn't been time to find cover anywhere else.

"Air pressure suddenly rose: my ears popped like coming down fast in a plane," remembered Dan. "Everything burned. The wet and icy mud coating me baked to clay. Many dirt clods fell and thumped on the ground. I put my hands behind my head to guard it. [My hands] began burning. I'd been wet and freezing, but seconds later felt dried as a prune."

A bit away from Dan, down, under the logs and trees, Brian had tried to stand up, but when he felt the heat, he had ducked back down. The logs giving him shelter had protected him from the worst of the blast.

As the air began to clear, Dan and Brian had shouted for each other. But the haze and debris muffled the noise. Neither man could hear the other.

Seemingly by himself, Dan headed for the river.

"Yesterday's icy clear water was now warm and thick with black mud and tree limbs. Even so it felt good on my burned hands," said Dan.

He stayed in for as long as he dared, but up above, "a big ash cloud way up flashed hundreds of red lightning bolts."

The eruption wasn't over yet. Ash and darkness were coming.

Dan scrambled up the riverbank and climbed onto a tree trunk.

"Brian!" he screamed.

There was no answer.

"Can *anyone* hear me?" he shouted.

This time, he heard Brian's voice calling faintly back, like he was shouting from far uphill.

Dan walked along the fallen tree trunk, trying to head back up to where the tents had been. Sixty feet along the logs, he fell.

"I slipped off and stuck out my elbows," said Dan. His arms caught on the logs. "As I hung between [the trees] a hand grabbed my foot! I looked down to Brian!—on the ground reaching up through limbs."

"My leg! My leg!" Brian screamed. "I think it's broken!"

"I gotta get you up!" Dan said.

They reached toward each other, but when they clasped hold, the skin on Dan's burned arms slid off.

Dan tried again. He gripped Brian's wrists and pulled, both men in nearly unbearable pain.

This time, they held on. Dan lifted Brian to the log, and they sat, together, as the ash brought darkness.

❋

Hours later, Sue and Bruce heard their cries for help and scrambled through the devastation to find them.

"Where's Terry and Karen?" Brian asked when only two of their friends appeared out of the haze.

"Trees fell on them," Bruce answered. "I think they're dead."

Just that morning, Terry had caught a fish so big that it made his line snap. It had been mere hours since that moment; it had been a lifetime. Before the darkness, before the heat, and before the ash.

Now, the friends—down to four—had to figure out how to survive.

Brian couldn't walk. There were downed trees in every direction, and it was impossible for him to climb up and over them with a broken hip.

Sue, Bruce, and Dan carried Brian to a demolished cabin thirty feet away.

"It was all they could do to get me those ten yards," Brian said. He begged them not to leave.

But someone had to survive. Someone had to go get help.

"*Someone* had to get out," remembered Bruce. "That meant us."

Dan gave Brian a long-sleeved shirt and then threw up "what seemed a gallon of ash," he remembered. The friends tried to make sure Brian had shelter. They tried to make him as comfortable as possible. He pleaded with them not to go.

But the cloud from the mountain was still rising in the distance. No one knew what was coming next. They needed help. They needed to escape. And that meant leaving Brian behind.

Six friends had begun the morning making a fire, fishing, sleeping in. By 11:00 a.m., the group who began walking out to find help was down to three.

CHAPTER 27

30 Miles Southwest

Mindy Brugman and Carolyn Driedger were on their way back to Mount St. Helens. They had woken up early that morning and attended the daily 7:00 a.m. staff meeting in Vancouver. When her request for use of the helicopter was denied, Brugman decided to drive back to the mountain with Driedger, determined to hike their way up to the glaciers and get more data.

Just before 8:30 a.m., barely a half hour outside of Vancouver, they pulled off to stop for gas and food. Naturally, they kept their eyes toward Mount St. Helens.

Then the view changed.

"I remember seeing a line going straight up [from] the mountain," Brugman recalled. "And low-ish clouds all around."

She called out, "Carolyn, look at that. The mountain's erupting."

Driedger looked. But the clouds were so far away. As much as they marred the horizon, she was certain it wasn't an eruption. "Oh, no, that's pollution from Longview," Driedger replied.

But Longview wasn't in that direction.

"Maybe they're doing a clear-cut?" Driedger suggested instead, thinking that Weyerhaeuser or the National Forest was taking down a section of trees.

Whatever it was, it was big enough that they could see it with their naked eyes from thirty miles away. A dark line, rising skyward.

Neither of them heard anything. Neither of them saw anything more.

They went into the grocery store, intending on getting food for the day. Inside, people were panicking.

"The mountain has erupted! The lava is coming!" shoppers were shouting.

Brugman and Driedger could easily dismiss that last fear—lava would never make it as far as the town.

But there were three dams between the mountain and them. If those were to break, then people actually would have something to worry about.

They ran back to their car. They had one of the USGS field radios. They tried to call David Johnston.

"It should've connected. But it couldn't connect to him," Brugman remembered.

So Brugman and Driedger found a pay phone and called the Vancouver office.

Don Swanson answered.

"The mountain has blown," he told them. "Please come back."

Their radio still wouldn't connect to Johnston. There was nothing they could do for him or the others at the mountain now. They couldn't change what had just happened, but they could, maybe, help prevent future tragedy. They were needed back in Vancouver.

But before Brugman left the phone, she made one more call. When her mother answered, the first thing Brugman said was "Mom: I'm alive. No matter what anyone says, I'm alive!"

"I didn't want for one second for [my parents] to think I had died," Brugman explained. Her parents and friends all knew she was working on the mountain—news of the explosions would surely travel fast, and she didn't want anyone to worry.

Her parents were still in bed when Brugman called so early on a Sunday morning. But her mother had woken up when the shock wave from the eruption rolled through Seattle. She watched the windows of their bedroom shake. Later, Brugman would find out that her brother, on the west coast of Washington, heard what sounded like eight explosions.

But within sight of the mountain, Brugman and Driedger—like everyone else within thirty miles of the eruption—heard almost nothing.

MAY 18–19, 1980:
LATE MORNING TO THE NEXT DAY

CHAPTER 28

11 MILES NORTH

"CAN I HAVE A DRINK?" ADAM SMITH ASKED HIS DAD.

They had stayed sheltered under a huge fir tree, at the base of a bluff eleven miles north of the volcano. Twice, Adam's dad, Buzz, had tried to leave the shelter of their tree and find a path to safety. Twice, Buzz had turned back after taking only a handful of steps away.

But by late morning, the ash had thinned somewhat. Buzz's flashlight now lit as much as fifteen feet, about the length of a small SUV, in front of them.

It was time to get moving.

"Ahhh," Buzz replied, sheepishly. "I poured it out. We'll get some along the creek."

Water was heavy to carry, and their plan before the eruption was to hike alongside plenty of rivers and streams. Why bother carrying it when water seemed to be everywhere? It had been a good idea at the time—but that was before the eruption.

Yet even the lack of water wasn't their biggest problem. Their most immediate concern was finding a way out. The trail was gone.

Most of the trees around them were still upright, but their tops had been sheared off in the blast. Huge sections of trunks had fallen all around them: "I don't know why we'd not been speared," remembered Buzz.

They didn't have a path, so Buzz decided to head north—away from the volcano. As they moved away from their camp, they realized just how lucky they had been. Out where the bluff hadn't offered its protection, trees were toppled like matchsticks. Soon, they were climbing over entire fallen trunks, heading away from the volcano and toward the river and water and safety.

But when they reached the river, there was no water.

"Just mud," remembered Buzz. "Nothing to drink. Pouring out the water had been a big mistake."

There was nothing they could do about that now. They just had to keep moving.

As a Weyerhaeuser logger, Buzz was familiar with working on and around huge trees. They found a trunk that bridged the river, and Buzz put one son in front of him and the other behind him, inching their way across to the north bank.

When they reached the other side, they climbed about 40 feet above the river, knowing that it could flood. Then they turned west. The trail might be gone, but the road had to be out there, somewhere.

The air continued to lighten. In "suspended ashdust like firesmoke," Buzz described, they could now see about 150 feet in front of them. Far more than they had been able to see since the eruption.

Buzz, Eric, and Adam fought their way over massive trunks and across stretches of debris.

"Where [the ash was] deeper than a few inches it was hot," remembered Buzz. "We had boots on, but after deeper pockets of hot ash we climbed on logs to cool our feet."

Through the ash and mud, dehydrated and scared, they kept moving.

They kept walking on.

CHAPTER 29

17 Miles Northwest

Dan was hiking in socks. He had run out of the tent earlier that morning in jeans and a shirt, but he hadn't had shoes. Now, they were nowhere to be found.

The three friends—Dan, Sue, and Bruce—had left Brian behind. He had broken his hip while sheltering under a tree. The shelter meant he had escaped with few burns, but the tree had rolled and pinned him so that his bone broke. Brian couldn't walk, and the friends knew they needed to find help.

Dan didn't have any broken bones, but he was suffering as much as Brian. He had weathered the blast in the open. His burns kept him in constant pain. And walking without shoes meant that every step into the ash was rife with fresh heat.

"Ash had slid off high banks and pooled on the road almost too deep to walk in, the bottom six inches were hot as hell," remembered Bruce, and he was wearing boots.

Dan, clad only in stocking feet, ran from log to log. He walked on top of fallen trees to cool off. Eventually, he remembered that "my socks filled with hot ash," so he took them off. "It was cooler barefoot."

They walked for an hour and half, with Dan running through the open spaces and the dogs (who didn't appear to be hurt by the hot ash buried underneath the surface) scampering alongside. They covered only two miles in that whole time.

"At this pace," Bruce said, "none of us would be out by dark. I didn't think either Brian or Dan would last overnight out here."

Then, as if the slow pace wasn't difficult enough, the three friends came to a two hundred-foot stretch with no logs.

"The ash is too hot for me," Dan said, knowing what that meant. He couldn't cross that blank expanse. He couldn't go on.

"It was hard to leave a friend," said Sue.

Dan went down the banks to the Green River. All he could do was sit and wait for rescue and be prepared to jump in the ash-filled water if another blast came along.

On the road, Sue and Bruce began walking again.

Sue's dog, Cody, and the puppies that had been Karen's walked alongside them, but everywhere else the road and what used to be forest seemed to be covered with animals dead and dying.

"Many little animal tracks ran in circles," said Sue. It was almost too much to bear. The sight of a small bird fighting for its life brought Sue to tears.

Then, in the midst of so many animals, an even stranger creature appeared: a human survivor.

Grant Christiansen had tried to drive to Camp Baker, a

Weyerhaeuser work station, to get tools, but his car had died. He had abandoned it and was trying to reach a group of people who he had overheard on his truck's CB radio.

Grant joined with Sue and Bruce.

The three of them walked on.

CHAPTER 30

ABOUT 20 MILES NORTHWEST

BUZZ GUESSED THAT IT WAS MIDAFTERNOON WHEN THEY FOUND the road. At the intersection of the road and the river, in the parking lot where they had left it the day before, they found Buzz's pickup truck, "mashed lengthwise by a tree," he remembered. It was crumpled and useless, not that they could've driven it out, anyway; the road was buried in ash and fallen trees.

Perhaps the most interesting thing about the parking lot were the other tracks. It was the first proof they had that other people had made it through the eruption alive.

Then in the opposite direction, from up the river, they heard a cry: "Helllp! Helllp!"

Buzz left Eric and Adam with the truck—and firm instructions not to move.

Just to the east, back the way they'd come, Buzz found Brian Thomas.

"Don't go," Brian begged when Buzz hiked to him. He had been alone for hours. "Don't leave me here."

"It'll do no good to stay," pleaded Buzz, echoing what Sue, Bruce, and Dan had told Brian a few hours before. "I could only keep you company. I've got kids with me. We need to walk out and send someone back."

"Others have gone for help."

"I can't stay. We'll find someone to come back," Buzz promised.

There was nothing else to do. The injured man was desperate, scared, and in pain. But the best that Buzz could do was get himself and his kids to safety and live to tell others where Brian was.

Buzz left and found the boys, right where he had told them to stay. They started walking again.

They were tired and thirsty. On their left, the Green River wound its way toward the Pacific Ocean next to them. It was fresh water—it *had been* fresh water hours before—but now it was clogged with ash and mud, an undrinkable slurry that simply marked the area next to the road without providing any relief.

"A burnt-wood odor hung in the air," Buzz remembered. When they stopped to rest, Buzz gave the boys some pancake syrup and fruit rolls.

Eventually, the ash-filled air thinned to a very light gray. They began to see signs of animals. They saw many, many tracks in the dirt and dust.

"Why didn't the birds fly away?" Eric asked.

"I don't know," Buzz told him. "But look: even birds and hornets are walking. That's how we'll get out."

They were tired. They were thirsty, dirty, and sore. But Buzz kept encouraging his boys on. They kept moving.

They stayed alive.

They walked and rested, walked and rested, for more than an

hour. They passed Soda Spring, which fed into the Green River, but there wasn't any drinkable water there, either.

Then, just past the stream, Buzz and the boys saw a pair of ash-covered socks hanging from a tree. And just past that, they saw tracks diverge from the road down to the river.

A man was sitting at the riverbank.

"Weeks ago," Buzz remembered, "I'd seen T-shirts printed I SURVIVED MOUNT ST. HELENS."

The T-shirts had been souvenirs for the tourists who came to see the now laughably small eruptions. Mere puffs of steam, compared to what they were surviving that day.

But when Buzz saw the man at the riverbank, he thought back to those shirts.

"Hey!" he called. "Hey! Survivor!"

A man turned around and trudged up to meet them. It was Dan Balch, who had been camping with five friends the night before and who had parked next to Buzz's truck in the parking lot.

"He walked up slowly," remembered Buzz, "filthy in ash, arms and shirt caked gray. We were all gray—Adam with streaks down his cheeks where tears had run and dried."

Buzz gave Dan a pair of tennis shoes he had in his backpack and fed him syrup with a fruit roll. With shoes on, Dan decided that he could walk once more.

They kept moving on.

"This far out," Buzz said, "the ash was fluffy, and every step stirred it up. So we wouldn't breathe in so much, we walked a hundred feet apart—I leading, the kids, then Dan."

But the day that had started out so peacefully wasn't about to let up—the mountain had more in store for them.

"About 4:30 a loud explosion came from the southeast and shook the ground way out here—like a big bomb in the distance. The mountain must've blown again. We picked up the pace."

Where in the morning the eruption had been silent except for the rush of wind before the blast, this time, they heard the explosion. But where that morning they had felt the effects of ash and heat, this time they felt nothing but the ground shaking.

They kept walking.

Dan was burned; he needed medical attention. All four of them needed water.

They had been hiking for hours, climbing up and over dozens of old-growth firs with trunks that were often wider than the boys were tall. They had been breathing in ash that coated their throats, the particles of dust sucking their mouth dry, just like it did the smaller springs that had fed into the Green River.

"I was sure Elk Creek, a big stream from the north, would be flowing," remembered Buzz. "But the ash had absorbed its water. It was chocolate-colored mud only [a] foot wide and inches deep."

A mile farther down the road, the place where Cascade Creek should've been, was dry as well.

Three hours after they met Dan Balch, the road crossed the Green River.

"[It] was still mud. But I spotted a seep down a bank. I brushed away ash and groundwater trickled out," remembered Buzz.

Adam drank half a cup. So did Eric. They each drank another portion.

The water was gritty. It was drinkable, but barely. The boys refused to drink any more.

While they were drinking, Buzz got his first, good look at Dan.

"Now I saw water oozing from his neck, and no skin! I looked him over. No skin on parts of his arms—not much hide elbows to fingertips! He'd been so caked in ash I hadn't noticed this," Buzz remembered.

"Man, you're hurt!" Buzz said to Dan. "You need to drink more water."

"It'll just make me throw up," said Dan.

"You're burned. You need to drink water even if you throw up."

Buzz went and got another cupful of water from the seep. It was ash-filled and scratchy, but it was water, and Dan drank it all.

"How'd you get so burned?" Buzz asked.

"Didn't you feel the heat?" Dan replied.

"Not *that* hot."

Buzz and the boys had hidden at the bottom of the fir and put the sleeping bag up as a shelter. They had camped at the base of a bluff. It was luck.

They hadn't been hit by falling trees. They hadn't choked on ash. It was luck.

They had survived. They had lived this long. They would keep going on.

And not a hundred yards after they had begun walking west

again, the roar of a military Huey helicopter flying low meant that they would make it out alive.

The helicopter had followed their tracks down the road. They'd been found.

The Huey landed ahead of them, and two crew members jumped out and met the group. They carried Eric and Adam—exhausted and dehydrated—back to the waiting helicopter. As the four survivors climbed in, a news reporter snapped their pictures.

One of the first things Buzz did when he arrived at the Huey was to tell the pilot and crew about the injured Brian Thomas. Just as he had promised, Buzz had made it out and made sure that Brian would be rescued as well. He had kept his word.

Ash flew up in a blinding white cloud as the helicopter tried to take off. Twice the crew had to set the helicopter down again and clear out air filters. On the third try, the pilot finally rose using his instruments alone—without being able to see anything out of the windows—to get them aloft.

When they could see once more, the crew cheered. It wasn't until Buzz, Dan, and the boys heard the crew's relief that they realized how dangerous the situation had been near the ground.

They flew over the flooding Toutle River and even over Buzz and the boys' house.

They touched down at Longview Hospital around 8:15 p.m.

Buzz, Eric, Adam, and Dan walked into the hospital on their own power, survivors to the end.

CHAPTER 31

About 27 Miles Northwest

SUE AND BRUCE WERE BOTH YOUNG—SUE WAS TWENTY-ONE YEARS old and Bruce was twenty-two. Grant "in his sixties with leathery dark skin seemed old," Bruce said. But the three of them continued on together, following what Grant had overheard on his truck's CB radio before it broke down: There might be people up the road, other survivors.

As they walked, Grant told them stories. He had been at the battle of Guadalcanal in World War II in 1942. He had been wrecked there, too, at sea in a lifeboat for two days before being rescued.

There was hope in his words, in his stories of survival, even if he was still suffering from the old wounds. "The old man's glass eye kept getting ashy," remembered Bruce. "He popped it out several times to wipe [it] off."

The words, the reminders of persistence, kept them moving on amid so much death and destruction.

They kept walking.

"Not long before dusk, a Huey helicopter flew near," remembered Bruce.

But all three of them were covered in ash. Their gray bodies and clothes blended in with the gray road and gray ground and gray trees. The pilot couldn't see them.

The helicopter began to fly away. Their chance for rescue was leaving.

"We shed our shirts and beat them on the ground," said Sue. "It raised the dust."

The whirr of rotors grew louder. The helicopter turned back. Their own cloud of ash rising from the ground had marked them as survivors.

It landed down the road, where the lane was wide enough, and two crew members jumped out to guide Sue, Bruce, and Grant back to the helicopter.

Pilot Mike Cairns leaned forward to hug Sue as she and the dogs climbed inside.

"We're *so* glad to see you!" he said.

"Not half as glad as I am," she replied.

It was 8:30 p.m.—almost exactly twelve hours since Mount St. Helens first erupted. They'd hiked fifteen miles.

When Sue and Bruce told the crew about Dan and Brian, the pilot immediately responded that Dan had already been picked up. But when they showed him on the map where they had left Brian, the pilot was incredulous.

"No one could be alive that far up," he cried, disbelieving that anyone could've come from that close to the mountain.

"*We* came that far!" Sue and Bruce charged.

"Okay," Cairns said, "we'll go."

Minutes later, they were circling the rundown shelter where they had left Brian.

But Brian was not there.

In such a large helicopter, they couldn't land to search for Brian themselves, but they called in another rescue chopper. When the second helicopter arrived, it managed to perch shakily on a one-lane bridge while a rescue crew jumped to the ground. Cairns flew in circles while the crew from the second helicopter searched below.

They couldn't circle forever.

"We're too low on fuel," said the pilot.

Sue had promised Brian they'd return. She had promised that they'd rescue him, too.

As he turned the helicopter toward safety, Cairns paused to listen to his radio. He reached out and grabbed Sue's arm.

"They got him!" he cheered.

The rescue crew had found Brian near the road, about two hundred yards from the cabin. He had left the shelter around noon, unable to take the stress of simply waiting alone. In eight hours, he had managed to crawl, flop, and drag himself the length of two football fields. Later, he would remember raising his head to look the rescue crew in the eye, but he had no memory of moving toward the helicopter or the flight to the hospital.

But he was found. He was safe.

Soon Sue and Bruce touched down with Grant Christiansen in Kelso, on the Washington/Oregon border, far south from the reaches of the eruption.

Finally, they were safe, too.

CHAPTER 32

IN THE AIR

DON SWANSON HAD BEEN PLANNING ON DRIVING TO THE mountain, but he quickly changed plans as soon as word of the eruption reached the USGS office in Vancouver. He boarded an airplane, instead.

An hour and twenty minutes after the mountain had first erupted, the cloud cleared enough for Don Swanson to get his first, sustained look at the top of what was left of Mount St. Helens.

"A roiling, dark column pumped and convected up as a high cloud looking like dirty cauliflower but every knob moving," he remembered. "A little knob grew to a huge one, this all over the outside of the column that rotated up to the right, a twisting helix. It looked very slow, but from its enormous size I knew it must be very fast . . . It towered miles above us, far larger than I'd imagined."

Then he looked down, to the base of the twisting, boiling plume.

"Incredible!" he breathed over the plane's radio. "The top of the mountain's gone!"

Later he would remember that "the views were so brief and fuzzy, a missing summit so unexpected, we were in denial about it."

"The rim was chopped off above Northwest dome, more than a thousand feet below yesterday's summit," he remembered.

The plume from the summit continued to rise the entire time Swanson and the crew flew around the volcano. Lightning flashed in the swirling mass for hours and hours.

They thought they had been prepared for it. Crandell and Mullineaux had looked back and described the worst eruptions in the past. But even their most dire predictions had been small in the face of the devastation around Mount St. Helens.

Swanson had question after question. "An isolated white steam plume puffed up . . . from near Spirit Lake . . . But what caused it?" To the east, "all trees [were] down, everything coated in gray ash, many dispersed small fires . . . How could ash falling through cool air set fires? Had lightning set them—but then why so many?"

At this point, they were four miles east of the crater, and it was unimaginable that the destruction could be this far out. And if it was this bad to the east, how terrible must it be to the north, where the landslide and blast had been focused? To the north, Swanson realized that the "devastation . . . must be huge."

They flew throughout the morning and early afternoon, taking pictures and video of the eruption that went on and on. All Swanson and the scientists could do now was watch and witness.

There had been no warning. They had hoped that more earthquakes, or perhaps a new growth on the bulge, would signal that the big one—the eruption they were all waiting for—was about to happen. Instead, it had come unannounced.

"I'd been measuring the mountain for weeks. We thought increased swelling and seismicity would herald a big event," said Swanson. "Yesterday we'd measured from a ridge just below and landed on the summit. Had it erupted then we'd be dead. Had [the morning's staff meeting ended] earlier I'd have been at Coldwater II. It could be Dave Johnston flying here now worried about me down there."

A brief quake on a beautiful morning, the same as so many other earthquakes on so many other mornings, had changed heaven to hell.

CHAPTER 33

IN THE LAB

"IF THAT ERUPTION HAD HAPPENED A HALF HOUR LATER, WE would've driven right in the path of the mudflows that came down," said glaciologist Mindy Brugman, echoing the same thoughts as Don Swanson up in the air. "There's a very good chance we would've been killed."

How many other people around the mountain were saying and thinking the same thing? There had been a staff meeting at the USGS offices in Vancouver that morning—how many scientists were alive at 8:33 a.m. because the meeting had run a bit long?

Brugman and Carolyn Driedger turned back as soon as they heard that the mountain had erupted.

"So we arrived [back] in Vancouver, and then everyone's kind of gone," remembered Mindy.

Swanson had left to fly to the mountain. Other scientists were either in the air or scattered in labs, trying to piece together what information they had coming out of the volcano. The usual leaders—Crandell and Mullineaux—were both absent. They had been working almost nonstop for weeks on end; they had needed a break. Mullineaux was in California to see his daughter graduate from college, and Crandell had gone home to Denver. They were only now beginning their trips back to Washington.

People were gone, but noise and confusion echoed throughout the office.

"The phones are ringing everywhere and . . . all I could hear were these radios going 'should we evacuate?' 'Is there a flood?' It was really terrible."

Through the chaos, with everyone else gone, Brugman and Driedger sat down to answer the phones and triage the information coming in.

CNN called. Local news called. Residents called. The USGS offices were flooded with people wanting to know what was going on and what they needed to do.

They took turns listening in on the radio conversations of the scientists flying over the volcano.

"I'd take notes," said Brugman, as she listened in, and then they'd discuss what they could tell the new reporters.

They turned over the information as soon as they had it. They advised people as best they could. They answered questions and soothed fears. And still the phones rang and rang.

It went on for hours.

＊

Since the mountain started shaking a month and a half before, there had been someone in Steve Malone's lab watching the seismometers and recorders twenty-four hours a day, every day.

At 8:32 a.m. on Sunday, May 18, the person on night shift was just handing the work over to the person on day shift. They watched as the recorder lit up with the earthquake that began it all.

"I was at home," Malone remembered, "eating breakfast."

He got a call from the lab. "Boy, we've just had a big, big earthquake. It's bigger than any one I've seen so far."

Malone left his food, jumped on his bike, and raced the two miles from his home to the lab.

When he got there, Malone remembered, "all of us in the lab were shook. Now what to do?"

They hadn't seen any signs of an imminent eruption in the seismic data. Was there something they had overlooked?

"I was quite concerned that we had missed something," Malone said, his simple words belying the deep emotion in his voice.

He and the other scientists looked back through their records.

"There wasn't anything out of the ordinary." He searched and searched, but "there wasn't a decrease, there wasn't an increase [in the number of earthquakes]. There hadn't been an unusual tremor . . . There was nothing out of the ordinary. This was just one more earthquake."

There wasn't anything they could've done. They hadn't missed a sign or signal, but that only added to a sense of helplessness. It was a relief entirely overshadowed by grief.

CHAPTER 34

NOTHING TO SAVE

IN A CAMOUFLAGED DARK GREEN AND TAN HUEY HELICOPTER, A
crew of pilot, co-pilot, flight engineer (who would operate the
250-foot power hoist), and two pararescue jumpers from the Air
Force Reserve 304th squadron touched down outside of Vancouver,
Washington. Designated Save 82, this crew was there to pick up
one more person: a geologist.

"I thought the USGS geologist we'd pick up was Dave Johnston
whom I'd arranged to fly with us in an eruption," pararescue
jumper Michael Cooney remembered. "But it was Harry Glicken."

For a single, fateful night, Johnston had been on the mountain.
Now Save 82 picked up a different person than they'd planned.
Harry Glicken stepped into the helicopter, and they took off. They
had one mission: to find and save the missing geologist.

They didn't know they were already far too late. None of them
were prepared for what they saw.

"Spirit Lake was all debris, the forested ridge just west was
barren. Truman's lodge and cabins among the firs were gone. Only
horizontal [fallen] logs and gray debris [remained]," remembered
Cooney. "We flew northeast. I saw patches of water ahead: The

lake was here, just covered. At Harmony Falls the big trees were gone, the area scraped clean. The tall lower falls were gone; the upper ones now dropped near the lake."

They were trying to find Spirit Lake but could only see glimpses of water beneath a flat area of debris. The whole landscape was entirely changed.

Coldwater II was gone.

They flew over the highway and saw burned cars with the bodies of people inside. Where they could, the pararescue jumpers collected purses and IDs.

"Smoke rose from burning timber," remembered Glicken.

As their fuel ran low, they flew to the makeshift staging area at Toutle High School, refueled, and took off again. An hour and a half later, they did the same once more.

Ruin met them each time they returned to the mountain. "I'd not have known there'd been a forest," said Glicken. "The crew said it looks like a nuclear blast. The valley was full of gray mounds ten yards high. Dark-brown mud braided through them . . . past occasional ice blocks. Three feet of ash covered downed trees."

"This is stupid," muttered Save 82 commander Major Peters after their third trip out. "Nothing to save."

They were courting danger—another eruption could occur, or a collision in the air with other helicopters masked in the ash, or even engine failure from churned-up ash on the ground—every time they flew near the eruption. The longer they flew, the more they exposed themselves to the potential for disaster.

No one, aside from Harry Glicken holding out desperate hope for Dave Johnston, thought of those as rescue flights. It seemed like they were putting themselves in pointless danger.

They weren't the only ones trying to help, either. The Coast Guard also had helicopters in the air, and Weyerhaeuser, too, put their helicopters to work in search and rescue.

There were so many people and planes and helicopters that there was more than one near-collision. Especially while landing and taking off, ash blinded the pilots. They flew close to the ground using instrument read-outs alone—they couldn't see anything outside their windows.

That afternoon, the air became so crowded that several helicopters landed in the fields around Toutle High School at the same time. Major Peters demanded to know who was in charge.

No one could tell him.

"Fine," Peters said. "I'm in charge. Get out your maps. Let's not run into each other."

They divided up the area and went back out again.

Later, when the erupting mountain showed an increase in the ash jetting from its top, the helicopters were all called back—it wasn't worth more death in a place where no one could've lived.

Glicken had ridden three times in helicopters, seeing the same view each time. But he couldn't give up on finding Johnston. He kept on, trying to convince Major Peters to fly in from the north— perhaps that direction would help them see Johnston or the trailer.

But by the third flight out, Major Peters had enough. He could see what Glicken refused to believe: Johnston was gone.

With flights grounded and no way to get to Mount St. Helens, Glicken went back to the USGS offices.

"I remember seeing Harry Glicken curled up in a dark corner at the Vancouver headquarters," said Brugman who was still staffing the phones late that day. "He felt it was his fault that David died on the mountain. He was totally devastated."

They were all devastated—one of their own had died. But for the luck of timing, it could have been any one of them. It could have been many more.

CHAPTER 35

FLOOD PART 1: SOUTH FORK

THE AVALANCHE, THE BLAST, AND THE ASH HAD COME AND DONE their worst. But the destruction from Mount St. Helens was not over yet.

The floods were coming.

It began not with an absence of noise or a deafening crush of earth, but with the gurgle of water and the alarm of a siren. This time, for this piece of the disaster, there was some warning.

Roald Reitan and Venus Ann Dergan were both in their early twenties and had taken a weekend trip to fish and camp along the South Fork of the Toutle River, twenty-six miles west of Mount St. Helens. Their tent was five feet above the river and thirty feet back from the water line. Their car was up a steep bank, another ten feet above them.

On Sunday morning, Roald woke to the high, then low, sounds of a warning siren.

He listened. The river sounded like it did any other day.

Five minutes later, he couldn't say the same thing. Now the water sounded like rapids.

"The river looked like chocolate milk," Roald said.

The water was dark with churned up mud and silt. Debris

began rushing by: first sticks, then branches, then entire trunks of trees.

"Venus!" he called. "Get up! Something's wrong with the river! We should get out of here!"

They rushed their tent and packs up the steep bank to their car. The water rose two feet as they made the trip.

"Suddenly, logs came down fast, bank-to-bank," said Roald.

The smallest ones were sixteen inches in diameter and twenty feet long. The river kept rising, and the higher it rose and the faster it ran, the bigger the logs it brought.

"Two minutes after the first logs passed, a structure came around a bend half a mile upstream. Trees on the south bank shook when hit hard . . . It was a wooden railroad trestle 50 feet long, 15 feet high. Logs stacked behind it were huge as Greyhound buses."

Behind the railroad trestle, the water spread even more, the rushing flood "snapping off trees like they were matchsticks . . . The earth shook, the snapping grew loud, and the air stank of trees."

In front of them, the trestle broke apart.

The river rose ten feet in fifteen seconds.

By this point, Roald and Venus were in their car, fifteen feet above where the river had been when they woke up that morning. The water was still rising.

"There was no place to run," said Venus. "We could hear trees snapping down."

"Big logs rolled with high momentum up onto the road in

front of the car," remembered Roald. "They jammed every which way, some sticking above the car."

What had been a brown river a few minutes before had changed to a thick slurry of debris. "Chocolate milk had become chocolate pudding," said Roald.

They were already on the highest bank, sitting in their car. But the mud reached them there, too. They got out and climbed onto the roof.

"It had been serene," said Venus. "Now it was the end of the world."

When the car began to float, Roald jumped.

He landed on a log and managed to straddle it, staying on top. But a big log on his right side pinned his leg at his knee. He was facing forward on the log, but the current was "bucking chaotically up and down."

"A branch underneath caught my left foot," he said, "and held. My left leg stretched back with force, while my right knee was being mashed between logs. The pain was intense. A smaller log rolled over from behind and knocked me flat . . . I laid face-down, the pain excruciating from my legs being mashed and stretched. I hoped the next log would kill me."

Instead, the branch holding his left foot prisoner loosened. Then the log on his right side eased away a bit, too. With both legs free, Roald crawled to the front of the log as it "bucked wildly in the current."

As he looked over the front of his log, fifteen feet away in the mud, he saw Venus.

"She kept going under."

"I was pulled along fast in the current down between logs," said Venus. "They squeezed together and caught the arm I was holding on with. It mashed my left wrist and tore skin away."

Roald screamed, "Hang on! Hang on!"

"His screaming kept me going," said Venus.

"I grabbed her arm and pulled," said Roald. "The logs were rolling and bouncing, the mud slippery . . . Twice I got her halfway up, twice I lost her."

"Again I floated between big logs, grasping anything floating to stay up. The logs were far too big to hold much," said Venus.

"She floated down between the sawed ends of two big ones . . . If the logs came together they'd squish her. They separated a little. Her hand came up and I grabbed."

This time, as Roald pulled, Venus landed on the log next to him.

The log was huge. Five feet in diameter, forty feet long—as long as a school bus. They rode on the side of the river, being swept downstream by the current.

In the middle of the river, where the water was moving faster, "Roald's car floated by like a boat," remembered Venus.

As they went under the South Fork bridge, the current began to slow. The river opened up this far down, and the mud and water slowed as it took up more space. Yet even in this wider section, the river was still rising; a port-a-potty—far back from where the riverbank had been that morning—was buried in the mud nearly to its top.

They climbed off the log when the river widened to meet a road.

"We'd been in the river five minutes," said Roald. "It seemed like five hours."

The water and mud had been warm. "I had expected a cold-water shock," Venus said, remembering when she first landed in the river, "but it was warm like bathwater, perhaps 80°F."

But after their five minutes riding on the log, being exposed to the air, "I felt cold," said Venus. "The mud dried fast, caking up before Roald could pull it off. It was heavy like cement."

Not only was the cold mud quickly draining heat from her body, the river was still rising. They were out of the water for the moment, but they weren't out of harm's way yet.

"It's surprising what you do when endangered. Though injured, we climbed," said Venus.

They scrambled up another slope and went barefoot—the river had taken their shoes and socks—through the forest back to the bridge. There hadn't been anyone on the bridge when they passed underneath, but by the time they stumbled into sight, a sheriff's car was on the road and people had gathered to watch the flood.

The crowd heard Roald and Venus's shouts.

They were two hundred feet below the bridge, surrounded by trees and bramble, and there wasn't a place for a helicopter to land. Men who had gathered to watch the river came down and began to cut away the brush as others rushed to call for help.

Soon, the whirr of rescue was heard overhead.

First Venus, then Roald, got into rescue helicopters flown by volunteers from Weyerhaeuser and were taken to a nearby hospital. Roald had escaped relatively unscathed, despite what it felt like the logs had done to his legs. But Venus was a different story.

"I was covered with mud dried like a cast. They said I looked like a mud statue," Venus remembered. "At the hospital, "they put me on [pain medication], washed me three times, and found my wounds . . . My left arm had torn open knuckle to elbow. The left wrist was broken—the one Roald had pulled me up onto the log by."

But they had survived Mount St. Helens.

CHAPTER 36

FLOOD PART 2: NORTH FORK

DONNA DUBETH HADN'T WANTED TO BE ANYWHERE NEAR Mount St. Helens.

After reporting on the volcano since March, she had packed up and headed back home. When the mountain blew, she thought the eruption was going to be big. She wanted no part of it.

Still, as hard as she'd tried to run from it, there was no escaping Mount St. Helens.

"An explosion awakened me in Seattle," she remembered.

The noise that had been missing for everyone near the volcano was apparent farther away, enough to jolt duBeth from her bed.

By early afternoon on Sunday, May 18, duBeth was on a helicopter above the ruined landscape with newspaper photographer Roger Werth, flying over the North Fork of the Toutle River. Dozens of miles away from the volcano, there was still plenty of destruction and devastation to report on and witness.

They couldn't believe what they saw.

"A churning wall of mud, trees, and debris swallowed Camp Baker, overturning bulldozers and trucks like toys," said duBeth. "Why such destruction so many hours after the eruption?"

The eruption might be smaller hours after the initial blast, but the rush of water was only beginning. The heat had melted huge sections of glacier, and the water had begun to flow downstream. It had gathered power as it went, adding more melting ice, water, mud, and wreckage.

"We flew down over houses and gardens by the calm river," remembered duBeth. "The muddy debris came and devoured them."

They out-flew the flood, moving ahead of the line that turned the river from peaceful to dangerous. Thinking that they could get a picture of the oncoming deluge, the pilot set down near the river. Werth jumped out of the helicopter.

"I ran to the bank five feet lower [than the helicopter] and clamped the camera to a tripod. I was composing a shot when I saw my feet *in* the mud! I dashed back to the helicopter," said Werth.

"He dove onto the seat, and I pulled him in by the belt. The mud came within a few feet before we got off," said duBeth.

The water was rising fast.

Farther down the river, logs piled against the concrete-slab Coal Bank Bridge. The water rose, the mud brought more logs, and the jam grew. Massive tree trunks, though they looked like toothpicks from the air, slammed again and again into the bridge.

"A loud squeal of steel 'eeeeeeeeeeeee!,' a white puff of pulverizing concrete, and the deck [of the bridge] broke loose," said Werth.

Another puff of white dust, and the other end broke free as well.

"The 500-foot span floated like a surfboard," said duBeth.

"One end shot up, the other slid back, and it vanished into the mud."

Toutle High School—the same place where Crandell and Mullineaux had briefed the residents about the destruction and power of the volcano only nine days before—was the staging area for helicopters and rescue efforts. It was high ground, and many residents had evacuated there when the high-low siren had alerted them that a flood was coming.

The Toutle residents, at least, had time to prepare. The flood that wrecked bridges also tore away homes and yards, but the people had time to escape.

CHAPTER 37

Mount St. Helens—May 18, 1980

Over time, scientists were able to piece together a complete picture of the eruption of Mount St. Helens.

It began on Sunday, May 18, 1980, at 8:32:11.4 a.m. Pacific Standard Time (PST), with a 5.1 magnitude earthquake when pieces of ice and dirt at the top of the mountain fell into the crater at the summit.

The first landslides and Spirit Lake

Fifteen seconds after the earthquake, the bulge on the north face of Mount St. Helens broke loose and began to slide down the mountain. Ten seconds later, a block of earth between where the bulge had been and the summit broke loose as well in a second avalanche.

The twin cascades of dirt, rock, ice, and water were the largest landslides ever recorded anywhere in the world. Pieces of rock sliding down the mountain were larger than skyscrapers. It was enough debris to bury the entirety of Manhattan forty stories deep. By the time the landslide reached Spirit Lake, it was moving at more than 100 miles per hour.

An 850-foot-tall wave surged up from Spirit Lake as the landslide crashed into it. Most of the water collapsed back, but a new bottom, formed from the dirt and rock of the landslide, had already been laid down by the time the water refilled the lake. The bottom of the new lake was 210 feet higher than it had been before.

As it flowed back, the wave of water dragged with it so many trees that a floating mass of logs covered the entire surface of the water. Rescue workers in the air that day initially wondered if the lake had disappeared, until they saw slivers of lake peeking through.

Before the eruption, Spirit Lake had flowed into the North Fork of the Toutle River, but the landslide dammed the lake. Debris from the landslide also dammed two creeks, South Fork Castle Creek and Coldwater Creek, and created two new lakes: Castle Lake and Coldwater Lake.

The blast

The mountain acted like a bottle of champagne, and the landslide was like removing the cork. With the sudden release of pressure as thousands of tons of rock fell away, groundwater flashed to steam and exploded out of the mountain. This lateral blast of steam and hot rock moved 670 miles per hour and was around 660°F.

Seventy-eight seconds after the earthquake, the blast reached Coldwater II.

The blast hugged the landscape as it moved, going up and over two ridges and spreading north, east, and west as it went. The blast toppled trees in a 230-square-mile area north of the volcano called the blowdown zone and left vegetation standing but seared lifeless—the scorch zone—on the edges.

The third landslide

Two minutes after the earthquake, a third landslide collapsed the summit of Mount St. Helens into its crater. This caused hot ash to roll down the mountain, covering an even greater expanse of land than the first blast. This second set of ash reached between ten and eighteen miles from Mount St. Helens and within six minutes had covered an area as big as ten Manhattans laid next to each other.

The combination of the summit's collapse and the first two landslides lowered the mountain thirteen hundred feet. In minutes, Mount St. Helens went from being the fifth highest mountain in the state to the ninety-second! The amount of dirt, rock, ice, and water removed from the mountain could fill a football stadium six hundred miles high.

The vertical eruption

Mount St. Helens erupted out of its top as well as out its side. In three minutes, this vertical plume had risen 35,000 feet. Six minutes after it began, the plume reached 60,000 feet, and by 8:50 a.m. PST, it was more than 80,000 feet high.

The cloud spread like an anvil, carrying ash somewhat west and north but concentrating the spread in the east. Places as far away as South Dakota reported ashfall from the cloud. Within two weeks, dust from the volcano propelled by wind had circled the globe.

The initial pyroclastic flow and blasts expired within minutes, but the vertical eruptions went on throughout the day. The plume gradually lowered until a subsequent eruption at 5:00 p.m. PST pushed it again to 63,000 feet before subsiding to 17,500 feet by 8:10 p.m.

Sound

Acoustic energy from the blasts was directed upward. This energy remained trapped in layers of atmosphere for twenty to thirty miles away from the volcano. This "cone of silence," which has since been noted in other volcanic eruptions, meant that anyone close to the mountain didn't hear the blast. Eventually, the trapped sound was refracted back down to the ground, sometimes hundreds of miles away. People as far away as British Columbia reported hearing "booms" and explosions.

Pumice, lahars, and floods

Around noon, pyroclastic flows of pumice and gases at about 1,300°F flowed down the mountain to the north and buried everything they touched in pumice up to 131 feet deep. This area was later named Pumice Plain. These flows did not reach as far away from the mountain as the earlier lateral blast, which had already killed almost everything living in the area of Pumice Plain. However, the heat of the pyroclastic flow at noon melted several glaciers and significantly added to the flow of water and mud that had begun earlier in the day.

The avalanche and blasts carried ice with them, and the heat from the volcano melted still more ice into water. After the eruption, groundwater that had been trapped in the mountain found paths to flow downhill. Lahars of mud and debris swept down the South Fork and North Fork of the Toutle River with reports of a twelve-foot wall of water, mud, logs, and buildings being pushed downstream. At one point, the flood measured fifty-three feet above the normal water line. The water moved as fast as twenty miles per hour.

Destruction

The energy released from Mount St. Helens was equivalent to four hundred megatons of nuclear explosives. But this energy was released throughout the day, so it was more like twenty-seven thousand Hiroshima-sized bombs going off one per second for nine hours.

All told, more than two hundred miles of roads, fifteen miles of highway, two hundred homes, and forty-three bridges were ruined. One thousand people were suddenly homeless. Hundreds lost their jobs when the forest was destroyed.

Fifty-seven people died.

MAY 1980–AUGUST 1982

CHAPTER 38

Working Through Grief

"I was *mad* at the mountain!" said Mindy Brugman, who had nearly camped at Coldwater II the night before the eruption. "I was mad that it killed people. I was mad that it was so ugly and dirty . . . I was mad at how dangerous it was."

"We'd failed," said Steve Malone, who had first recorded the earthquakes on Mount St. Helens. "For two months we'd counted and located thousands of earthquakes, looked for changes to anticipate an eruption. Then it just happened. It killed many people. It killed David Johnston. We could hardly work."

Carolyn Driedger, who had been with Mindy Brugman at Coldwater II the day before the eruption remembered that "it wasn't just a matter of 57 lives being lost, but it was the mental fragility and emotional fragility of everyone who had assumed this was a stable planet . . . There was a lot of sadness. But it is also a recognition that a lot of work had to be done."

There was so much grief and trauma. Yet if the scientists let their emotions get in the way of learning from the volcano, then the missed opportunity—the chance to prevent harm to someone else in the future—would only add to the tragedy.

Everything had changed on that Sunday morning at 8:32 a.m.

Now they had firsthand accounts that volcanoes could—and did—erupt with violent lateral blasts as well as vertical blasts. Mullineaux would later tell a Senate committee that "the lateral blast extended about three times farther than any such blast recorded by the geologic history of the volcano."

All of the hazard maps had been drawn using evidence from previous eruptions. Crandell and Mullineaux had used records of the past to predict what would happen in the future. Six people had died at the roadblock along Spirit Lake Highway. Had they anticipated such a large, lateral blast, the roadblock never would've been set up the same way.

"Our worst-case scenario was far, far exceeded," Malone said. "The hazard experts thought the blast might extend ten kilometers [6.2 miles]: it went thirty [18.6 miles], instead."

Voight's paper had stated the possibility, even likelihood, of a landslide. But even if that had been accepted as the one and only truth, it might not have been enough. There was so little known about lateral blasts that the damage was far worse than anyone had anticipated.

"We'd had two months of warning, but nothing on a socially useful timescale, where you can react and do enough. Months are too long, and seconds are too short," said Malone.

It was luck that many more hadn't died.

If Mount St. Helens had erupted twenty-four hours later, the forest would have been filled with Weyerhaeuser loggers back to their work week, instead of the few private contractors who had been killed while working on a weekend.

If the mountain had erupted two hours after it did, the convoy of property owners and managers, news crews, and law enforcement that was scheduled to repeat its journey to Spirit Lake would've been killed just as quickly as Harry Truman.

If the volcano had erupted even an hour later, many more scientists would've been within the devastated area.

It was luck, and the persistence of Crandell, Mullineaux, Johnston, Malone, and those with them to persuade the public to stay as far back as it had. Their science couldn't predict exactly when or how or where the mountain would erupt, but it did prevent many thousands of people from being closer to the mountain. Crandell and Mullineaux's warnings of floods enabled the residents along the Toutle River to be prepared to move to higher ground and prevented many lives from being lost in the flood. It was luck and the persistence of a few, making the most of the science they had to go on at the time.

But that didn't stop the blame from starting almost immediately after the volcano erupted.

CHAPTER 39

BLAME GAME

BY TUESDAY, TWO DAYS AFTER THE ERUPTION, GOVERNOR RAY had already decided on the stance she would take: "Many people chose to remain close to the mountain," she said at a press conference. "We cannot be responsible . . . It's a free country."

The politicians willingly passed the blame onto the victims.

It was a bald lie.

Only three people had been in the Red Zone at the time of the eruption: two civilian scientists and Harry Truman. Everyone else had been behind the no-go line.

After the eruption, President Jimmy Carter decided to pay a visit.

The Washington National Guard was exhausted from the rescue and cleanup efforts that they had been running in the days since the eruption. But on Wednesday, Chief Warrant Officer Chuck Nole was asked to help direct the president's flight around the mountain.

"The National Guard allowed us [to have] long hair, and with all the volcano flying, I'd slept at base. I'd no warning before the colonel's call [to help with the President]," remembered Nole.

But suddenly, he wasn't in an emergency situation anymore.

Instead, he was "a 36-year-old unshaven woolly-headed Guardsman in wrinkled flight suit and scuffed boots" facing "a cadre of handsome, young Marine officers—the President's elite fliers: close-cropped, fresh-shaved, immaculate in tailored flight suits, spit-shined boots."

Against this contrast, Nole had to tell them that they didn't know how to fly around Mount St. Helens.

"Their maps won't work in the changed valleys," Nole remembered. In the rain, cloud cover would add to their disorientation.

The eruption had changed the land around Mount St. Helens so drastically that it had to be relearned all over again.

The next day, a convoy of Army and Marine Huey helicopters flew the president, the governor, several senators, the Secret Service, and many reporters up and down the area that used to be forest and now was bare wasteland.

At the press conference after his flight, President Carter voiced his astonishment: "I've never seen or heard of anything like this before. Somebody said it looked like a moonscape. But the moon looks like a golf course compared to what's up there . . . You can't see where the ground was, formerly. The ash is several hundred feet deep. There are tremendous clouds of steam coming up. There are enormous icebergs, big as a mobile home. A lot of them are melting, and as the icebergs melt . . . the ash caves in and creates enormous craters . . . It's an unbelievable sight."

But then President Carter echoed Governor Ray's sentiments:

"One of the reasons for the loss of life that has occurred is that tourists and other interested people, curious people, refused to comply with the directives issued by the governor, by the local sheriff, the State patrol, and others. They slipped around highway barricades and into the dangerous area when it was well known to be dangerous," he said at another interview during his visit.

The president was wrong.

The simple fact was that the deaths from the eruption of Mount St. Helens were tragic. It was no one's fault.

James Scymanky, a logger who had been working in the area around Mount St. Helens during the eruption, had managed to survive while the three partners who were with him that morning died. He remembered that "we were miles outside restricted areas and carried Weyerhaeuser permits."

None of these men—the one who lived or the three with him who had died—were doing anything illegal. In fact, they had specific permission to be where they were.

But that answer, and the idea that science evolves and that sometimes there is no way to predict the future, was uncomfortable. It was much easier to blame people who couldn't speak for themselves.

CHAPTER 40

WHAT NOW?

LIFE, AS IT DOES, WENT ON.

The scientists kept working through their grief. The politicians kept talking, assigning blame—mostly to the victims and never to themselves. The mountain, of course, kept standing as well. It had changed completely, but neither fire nor water could make the mountain disappear. What to do with it now?

Just as they had before the eruption on May 18, everyone had thoughts and voices about what should be done. Susan Saul was adamant that her voice should be heard as well.

For decades, long before Mount St. Helens made international news, there had been a push to conserve the old-growth forest and natural land before the loggers felled the last of it. In 1980, Susan Saul was co-chair of the Mount St. Helens Protective Association, which was finally gaining ground and convincing the public to conserve the land.

After the eruption, faced with a blunted, blank landscape, Susan's group didn't quite know what to do. What was left to protect? But in October, Susan was invited on a tour of the devastated area, and what she saw hardened her resolve to defend the land once again.

Weyerhaeuser was already removing downed trees from the area.

Susan left the tour aghast. At the rate they were going, it would take less than two years for Weyerhaeuser to remove all the logs . . . and then what? It would mean that the land would go right back to the way it was: commercial licenses and logging to private companies.

"Land management decisions are being made with the bull-dozer and chainsaw," Susan told reporters after her visit. She was determined that the land should be preserved rather than exploited.

By the summer of 1981, there were three proposals for a national monument before the US Congress: one from Susan's group, one from the Forest Service, and one from Washington's new governor, John Spellman.

Over the next year, Susan Saul and the Mount St. Helens Protective Association were called on many times to help decide exactly which acres were the most important to preserve. In the end, a national monument was centered around the cra-ter and Spirit Lake with arms extending both north and south. Remaining old-growth trees as well as the devastated area were preserved.

David Johnston's friends and coworkers had started calling the ridge where he died "Johnston Ridge" soon after the erup-tion. In the years that followed, the Johnston Ridge Observatory was built there as a formal part of the national monument. It was a place for tourists to engage with the geologic history of the mountain, hear eyewitness accounts of the eruption, and act as a gateway to hiking trails. Johnston's sacrifice was not forgotten.

The bill that established the national monument and resulted in the Johnston Ridge Observatory not only set aside land but also charged the Forest Service to administer the area in a unique way. The bill specified that the Forest Service "shall manage the Monument to protect the geologic, ecologic, and cultural resources, in accordance with the provisions of this Act, allowing geologic forces and ecological succession to continue substantially unimpeded."

They were going to leave the mountain alone.

TODAY

CHAPTER 41

Life, Once More

Life seemed to have been obliterated from the blast area.

Charlie Crisafulli was an ecology student at the University of Utah when he first saw the blast zone in July 1980. He remembered a "very discrete, abrupt, shockingly abrupt, transformation from verdant forest to just gray and levelled . . . it was oh, my God. This is like how do you even fathom what had happened here? How can this be? It's so vast. It was so intense that it was chilling."

Immediately after the eruption, it seemed like everything—all plants and animals—had died. But just as the timing of the eruption saved the lives of many people, the timing of the eruption also saved many animals. In mid-May, much of the countryside at higher altitudes was still covered in snow. Animals, like pocket gophers, deer mice, shrews, voles, and other small mammals, were still in their winter burrows. The eruption killed many of them. But not all.

"We refer to these as epicenters of survivorship," Crisafulli said, who finished his degree and came back to Mount St. Helens to work for the Forest Service.

When these animals emerged, they survived by eating buried

roots and bulbs. They dug in the ash, mixing it with the soil, preparing the area for the possibility of new life to grow once more.

These small animals, who linked the "before" of the mountain to the "after," played an important role even once they had died. Scavengers could come and eat the dead animals, and what was left of their bodies would decompose and enrich the soil.

Roger del Moral, another ecologist, remembered a hike he took only four months after the eruption: ". . . far from any visible vegetation, I discovered an isolated, yet active ant nest."

It was only a nest of ants, normal many other places in the world. But high on "a dry and barren mudflow, 5,000 feet up on the slopes of Mount St. Helens," del Moral remembered, it was more like a miracle.

How did the ants survive? What were they eating? It must have been something below the mud and ash—but what?

". . . I could not determine whether soil animals or fungi were involved," wrote del Moral. "Despite my curiosity, I decided that my ignorance was less important than the existence of this microcosmic ecosystem in a veritable desert."

Understanding *how* the precious ants were surviving was less important than the fact that they *were* surviving. Del Moral's presence was clearly not needed or wanted.

"The ants were adding nutrients to the mud and hastening the reestablishment of less ad hoc food chains," he wrote.

Even the smallest of animals were playing their part, finding a way to survive, rebuild, and grow.

It wasn't just on land that this was happening, either. Spirit Lake, decimated by the avalanche, blast, and debris field, was initially unrecognizable to those who had known it before the eruption.

When Charlie Crisafulli first saw the lake, he remembered that "the water was warm and bubbled with new hot springs. The once famously clear water turned to murk. If you put your fingers in . . . you couldn't even see your fingertips. The whole area was gray and foul. It was putrid and smelled like rotten eggs."

If any fish had managed to survive the eruption, they didn't last long—bacteria began to grow rampantly in the hours after the lake was changed forever. The bacteria consumed what oxygen was in the water, and whatever animals were still living in the lake quickly died. Ecologists estimated that the eruption killed around eleven million fish.

It took three years, but in 1983, Crisafulli found evidence that the first microscopic plants had begun to colonize the lake. He guessed that they had been blown in by the wind or perhaps brought by birds. However they had gotten there, Spirit Lake was now their home, and their photosynthesis was creating oxygen as a waste product. The phytoplankton, microscopic plants that float near the surface of water, had begun to remodel the lake into an environment that could once again sustain larger life.

One of the most important discoveries of watching the land around Mount St. Helens was that nature had a way of taking care of itself. Life returned best if just left alone.

It was natural to want to try to "clean up" and "fix" the area. Some scientists even tried on a slice of land around the volcano. Their efforts failed.

Planes were hired to drop grass seed across a section of devastation. Mostly, the grass didn't grow. The mice population, however, exploded. With an abundant food source in the seeds, mice were drawn to the area. But it wasn't a natural food source, and eventually the seeds ran out. Hungry mice then began to gnaw on whatever they could find, often eating young trees that were fighting for their own survival. The mice killed the trees, and then, when those ran out, died themselves.

Not only did the re-seeding fail by not generating much grass, it also created an environment where the natural growth that was occurring—the trees—were destroyed in the process.

Nature worked best and recovered most successfully when left to its own methods.

"It has to be a lesson of resiliency," Crisafulli said. "One, our expectation is most life—albeit if there's just a few individuals—will persist. That's the first. The second is if you just leave nature alone, the systems will come back in really remarkable ways."

In 2024, more than four decades after the eruption, Mount St. Helens is green once again. Though there is still a raft of floating logs that moves from one side of the lake to the other as weather and wind push it, fish have returned to Spirit Lake as well. Conifers have started to grow again. After decades of mixing with the soil underneath and becoming enriched by animal and plant decomposition, the ash and mud were finally able to support large plants.

These conifers, though still small, have started to produce pine cones—seeds to help spread more plant life and return the forest to an area once again filled with towering trees.

"Each time I would come out here there would be a surprise, something would be unveiled," Crisafulli said.

The devastation wrought by the eruption on May 18, 1980, was not the final word for life in the area. Plants and animals found a way to rehabilitate the land around Mount St. Helens, and the ecologists and scientists studied all they could.

Mount St. Helens had surprises at every turn. Violent, like the blast, or gradual, like recovery, the area was a master class in the possibilities of Earth.

And it wasn't done yet.

CHAPTER 42

MOUNT ST. HELENS TODAY

THE ERUPTION ON MAY 18, 1980, WAS THE BIG ONE. BUT IT WASN'T the only one.

Over the summer of 1980, five more eruptions sent plumes of ash into the sky. Then, beginning in December 1980, a lava dome in the middle of the new summit crater began to grow. It kept building for almost six years until it reached a height of nearly one thousand feet.

Avalanches regularly fell from the crater walls. Snow accumulated on top of the dirt. Shadowed by the rim above for most of the year, a new glacier began to form. Crater Glacier, created around the lava dome on Mount St. Helens, was the newest and only flowing glacier in the Cascades.

Then finally the mountain went quiet.

For a while.

In September 2004, earthquakes began to swarm again, eerily like the ones in March and April 1980. A welt grew in the volcano's crater. Scientists began to warn of another eruption.

On October 1, 2004, it happened. Ash and gasses once more jetted into the sky from Mount St. Helens. The volcano that had never really gone to sleep was awake and angry once more.

Lava began to emerge from the welt.

For the next three years, the lava ran down in spines and pooled to create another dome, just to the south of the one that had been built up more than two decades before. The new dome pushed Crater Glacier to the north, down the funnel that had been created during the May 18, 1980 eruption. The glacier moved more than five feet per day while the lava dome was growing.

Today, the two lava domes sit side by side in the crater of the mountain. New growth has mostly stopped since 2008. Both of the new domes, together, replace less than 10 percent of what the May 18, 1980 eruption—the big one—had blown away.

For now, Mount St. Helens seems to be quiet once more. How long that will last, no one knows.

The USGS monitors all the volcanoes in the United States; its classification of the threat potential of Mount St. Helens is at the most dangerous: a very high threat potential.

It's easy to forget that Mount St. Helens is young, in terms of the ages of rocks and mountains. "Most of Mount St. Helens we see today [and before the 1980 eruption] is younger than the pyramids of Egypt," said Carolyn Driedger.

It's not a matter of *if* Mount St. Helens will erupt again—it's a question of when, and will we be ready?

CHAPTER 43

A Stethoscope on the Volcano

"In those days, weeks, months, years, now decades since 1980, Mount St. Helens has become the master teacher—an ideal lab for volcano studies," said Carolyn Driedger. "Imagine if . . . the mountain—any mountain—you're trying to study, all of a sudden the guts are torn from it so you can see the entire interior with all the evidence of previous eruptions laid out in the rocky layers like pages of a book. It's a fantastic learning opportunity."

One of the most important parts of taking that opportunity was getting the scientists in one place. The Cascades Volcano Observatory (CVO) in Vancouver, Washington, was founded officially as a USGS office in 1982. Today, it monitors sites throughout Washington, Oregon, and Idaho.

Scientists at the CVO today continue the work begun by the scientists working around Mount St. Helens during the 1980 eruption. Like Crandell and Mullineaux, CVO scientists examine rocks from previous eruptions—using the past to help predict what might happen in the future. Like Brugman, Swanson, and Johnston, CVO scientists also monitor active volcanoes through ground deformation, seismic activity, and gas emissions. Like Brugman and Driedger, who spent the hours after the eruption tending the phones and radios, the CVO continues to communicate with the public.

And, like Brugman bringing in the ruby laser ranger and Voight adding his knowledge of landslides, the CVO is constantly updating their tools and developing new ones.

"We don't know what we can't detect," said Seth Moran, chief seismologist at the CVO. Scientists are limited to studying the information that their instruments record; creating more accurate, more precise instruments is one of the CVO's main jobs.

Since 1980, an important tool has become the ability to remotely monitor volcanoes from space using satellites.

At the CVO, the scientist-in-charge, Jon Major, described that "there are satellites now that basically take radar images of the ground at repeat cycles. When you compare those images, you can see whether the ground is changing or not."

The scientists in 1980 measured the growth of the bulge over time from the Timberline and Coldwater II sites; scientists today are doing the same but collecting the information via satellites from space. Besides keeping people farther away from harm, a big advantage of this is the ability to monitor a greater number of places. Not only are known volcanoes and known hazards being watched, but radar from satellites is being used to monitor land that has not displayed volcanic activity as far as we know, but might one day.

In Oregon, there is a cluster of volcanoes called the Three Sisters. The landscape just to the west of the Three Sisters is forested, relatively flat terrain. But "from the late 1990s until now—it's still going on—the ground surface has lifted up about a foot over about a 12-mile diameter circle," said Major. "This isn't anything you would detect, walking on it."

The deformation to the west of the Three Sisters doesn't pose a problem right now, and it might not for a *very* long time to come. But the point is that the scientists are watching, and they're able to detect even these small changes.

Remote monitoring and satellites are also important when information is cut off from the rest of the world. When Hunga Tonga-Hunga Ha'apai erupted in January 2022, the island nation of Tonga was largely disconnected from the rest of the world. Internationally, scientists were left with only remote monitoring options.

However, the information from the satellites paired with instruments in other countries gave scientists enough of the story to help predict when and if tsunamis would arrive as well as a basic understanding of the extent of the damage.

Monitoring, both remote and local, is vital to saving lives.

"What we're trying to do with our instrumentation," said Major, "is to understand what is typical behavior of these volcanoes . . . And then, once we get a better understanding of what's normal, then we look for the unusual."

The unusual, the unexpected and different, will point to the next hazard. Both false alarms and true warnings will be improved by knowing the difference between a bad day on the mountain and a positive signal that a volcano is on the brink of eruption.

Today, the USGS and the University of Washington continue

to work together to keep an eye on Mount St. Helens. The partnership makes Mount St. Helens one of the most-instrumented volcanoes in the world.

"It's like having a stethoscope on the volcano," said Harold Tobin, Steve Malone's successor at the University of Washington.

Not only is there more instrumentation on the mountain today than there was in 1980, the instruments themselves have improved. Computer technology has also allowed an entirely different level of analysis for data from the volcano.

"Back in 1980," explained Janine Krippner, a volcanologist who has done research on the pyroclastic flows on Mount St. Helens, "you had these seismographs printed on paper."

Today, the data that were drawn onto paper are directly captured by a computer instead.

"The methods of working with that data to really tease out the important information have come a very, very long way," Krippner said.

With more instruments and better instruments, with strengthened partnerships, and with new technology from software to satellites, the story of Mount St. Helens erupting right now would be very different than in 1980. Just as Crandell and Mullineaux knew, taking lessons from the past—even the recent past—and combining those with what we are learning today, will help keep us safe tomorrow.

EPILOGUE

THE STORY SCIENCE TELLS

WHEN A CATASTROPHE HAPPENS, "YOU'RE DESPERATE FOR INFOR-mation," said Janine Krippner. "We've all experienced that with this [COVID-19] pandemic. You want *any* kind of information."

Steve Malone, too, compared Mount St. Helens to the pandemic. "Particularly in the early days of [the pandemic]," he said, "in which the scientists . . . sort of understood something about what this type of virus could do, but not a lot . . . reminded me very much of the early days of Mount St. Helens. When the scientists vaguely knew something about what was going on and what could happen."

Scientists are often experts in their field, the ones who know which instruments to use and what the data from those instruments mean. But their knowledge is useless if they can't communicate what they know to the larger world—and equally useless if the larger world won't, or can't, listen.

"It is critical that we work with social scientists," said Krippner. "Because that's where we take our core science into society to actually help people with it."

When our world changes—from a volcano or from a virus—we want to know how best to survive. With the advent of social media there are many more ways to spread information than there were in 1980. But are scientists able to write their stories in forms that non-scientists understand?

Scientists have their own language of concepts, methods, and numbers. But when there's an emergency, their discoveries will only help if they can communicate in a way that non-scientists can grasp. It is imperative that scientists learn how to describe their work to the larger world.

It is equally imperative that when scientists present their work, people listen.

Mount St. Helens erupted catastrophically more than forty years ago, but hazards to humans will never disappear. Science will continue to evolve, and scientists will continue to stretch the bounds of what we know. Learning how to listen to science and developing ways to communicate the story spelled in numbers and data, is a challenge put to us all.

LESSONS LEARNED

The eruption of Mount St. Helens on May 18, 1980, dramatically changed the way we understand volcanoes. These are some of the most important lessons learned:

Landslides and collapses are dangerous volcanic events

The initial landslide on the north slope of Mount St. Helens released pressure that had been building within the volcano, "uncorking" the mountain and giving an escape to the devastating blast. One of the major lessons learned on May 18, 1980, is that landslides—often called "collapses" by volcanologists—are not only possible but common. The pattern of hummocks in the debris fields around Mount St. Helens after the eruption helped scientists to recognize the signs of landslides at other volcanoes. Scientists now accept instability of volcanoes as a major hazard.

Lateral blasts can direct danger along the ground

The lateral blast at Mount St. Helens left such a thin layer of debris that "without eyewitnesses and all the downed trees, it might have been impossible for geologists to say for sure what exactly happened," said Carolyn Driedger. The eruption of Mount St. Helens was the first time that scientists had a clear picture of a lateral blast. Because it was well recorded, both in film and in eyewitness accounts, volcanologists gained an understanding of what a blast from the side of a volcano, rather than from its top, might do.

Records of a volcano's history are a bare minimum

Rocky Crandell and Don Mullineaux had done an excellent job detailing how Mount St. Helens behaved in previous eruptions. However, on May 18, 1980, scientists saw devastation that went far beyond the historical traces. Volcanologists learned that past behavior of a volcano can only be treated as a bare minimum in hazard assessment. There is always a possibility of a more catastrophic eruption than what the rocks have recorded.

Accurate forecasts of volcanoes are possible

Using what they learned from the eruption on May 18, 1980, scientists were able to show that studying ground deformation, gas composition, and seismic activity could lead to accurate forecasts of future eruptions. In the decade following the catastrophic eruption of Mount St. Helens, scientists accurately forecasted fourteen subsequent eruptions to within days or weeks.

Volcanoes—even dormant ones—need to be studied locally by a range of scientists

The USGS was quick to establish an office in Vancouver, Washington once Mount St. Helens began shaking and erupting in March 1980. In the month and a half between the first signs and the catastrophic eruption, hundreds of scientists worked to try to understand what was happening. After the eruption, the

Cascades Volcano Observatory was formally established in Vancouver, Washington in 1982, and other offices quickly followed: the Alaska Volcano Observatory, the California Volcano Observatory, and the Yellowstone Volcano Observatory. These offices employ and coordinate scientists who study a wide range of subjects: seismology, volcanology, glaciology, ground deformation, gas composition, geochemistry (chemistry pertaining to the earth), geophysics (physics pertaining to the earth), computer science, computer-based mapping, remote sensing, science communication, and social sciences.

Scientists now know that even volcanoes that aren't active to the naked eye have vents and pathways that may seethe under the surface. By using the wealth of skills and expertise gathered at the different volcano observatories, teams of experts work together to keep watch and send warning when a dormant volcano is about to become active.

More than scientists need to prepare for an eruption

The May 18, 1980 eruption of Mount St. Helens showed the need for a wide range of professions—from emergency responders to infrastructure specialists (people who work with water and sewer systems, electrical grids, dams, and ports) to news media—to understand the impact of volcanoes within their area.

While this preparation often happens at a local level, the international Volcano Disaster Assistance Program was created as a direct result of the Mount St. Helens eruption. Led by the USGS, this coalition helps not only to monitor volcanoes around the world but also works to train local scientists and emergency responders to prepare for an eruption.

ACKNOWLEDGMENTS

I WAS FORTUNATE TO BE ABLE TO INTERVIEW MANY OF THE scientists and figures quoted in this book and others who provided a wealth of information. I am deeply indebted to them for their time, patience, and careful explanations.

Particular thanks go to Steve Malone, Mindy Brugman, and Carolyn Driedger for their accounts of the science leading up to the eruption, their firsthand recollections of the day, and their thoughts on the forty years since—thank you! Thank you to Gary Kribbs, Janine Krippner, Freya Liggett, Harold Tobin, and Jon Major for all the information, papers, diagrams, and insight you provided. Thanks to Nick Heeb for his research and explanation of the aeroacoustics of the eruption, and for taking time away from hamburgers and hot dogs to ask if I understood it all.

To the team at Holt BFYR, Carina Licon, Ellen Duda, Lelia Mander, Jie Yang, Kylie Byrd, and Matt Stevenson, thank you for turning these words into a book. I'm consistently blown away by the work and inspiration that goes into publishing.

Brian Geffen, you amaze me! The way you see stories is incredible. I'm so grateful to have you as an editor—thank you!

Michael Bourret, thanks for hearing and talking through every idea that comes into your inbox. Your support and insight make the process so much smoother.

Tracy Vonder Brink, Andrew Speno, and Rebecca Morris, you're the best critique partners an author could ask for. These stories would be in a much messier state (and so would I!) without you.

Mom, you've done more editing via text message than one would think possible, and I have such a good time with each and every conversation. To you, Dad, Nika, Hilary, and Katya, thank you for never blinking when I said I wanted to be an author and standing with me every step of the way.

Adam and Lydia, getting to share more of my writing with you with each book is a joy. I'm glad you love volcanoes as much as I do! For what it's worth, Adam, Steve Malone absolutely agrees with your advice that "when a volcano erupts, you should not be around it."

Dominic, thanks for listening to all of the twists and turns of publishing. You make the best paper airplanes of anyone I know.

BIBLIOGRAPHY

"1980 Cataclysmic Eruption." n.d. U.S. Geological Survey. Accessed April 17, 2022. usgs.gov/volcanoes/mount-st.-helens/1980-cataclysmic-eruption.

Ammons, David. 1994. "Obituary: Dixy Lee Ray Dies: Past Washington Governor, Head of Atomic Energy Commission, Was 79." *Lewiston Tribune.* January 3, 1994. lmtribune.com/obituary-dixy-lee-ray-dies-past -washington-governor-head-of-the-atomic-energy-commission-was/article _bd5d2d15-46ec-554c-8fcb-89a3ebfe2de4.html.

Andrews, Robin George. 2021. "Why the U.S. Once Bombed an Erupting Volcano." *National Geographic.* October 27, 2021. nationalgeographic .com/science/article/why-the-us-once-bombed-an-erupting-volcano.

Arne. 2010. "Earthquakes, Mount St. Helens, and the May 18, 1980 Eruption." *Chronicling the Nisqually Earthquake and Other Northwest Quakes* (blog). March 22, 2010. nisquallyquake.wordpress.com/2010/03 /22/earthquakes-mount-st-helens-and-the-may-18-1980-eruption/.

Associated Press. 1980. "Mount St. Helens Blows Its Top." *Lewiston Morning Tribune,* March 28, 1980. news.google.com/newspapers?id=CLdeAAAAI BAJ&pg=4395%2C10406076.

Bendixen, Michael. 2021. "A Mount St. Helens Ecologist Spent His Life Researching the Volcano. Science Is Reaping the Rewards." Oregon Public Broadcasting. July 21, 2021. opb.org/article/2021/07/21/scientists -reaping-rewards-of-ecologist-mount-st-helens-work/.

Berkes, Howard. 2020. "'It Seemed Apocalyptic' 40 Years Ago When Mount St. Helens Erupted." *NPR,* May 18, 2020, sec. The Picture Show. npr.org/2020/05/18/854829288/it-seemed-apocalyptic-40-years -ago-when-mount-st-helens-erupted.

Blumenthal, Les. 1985. "Northwest's Dynamite Keg: Mt. St. Helens Is Still Now But May Be Building Toward More Eruptions." *Los Angeles Times.* March 31, 1985. latimes.com/archives/la-xpm-1985-03-31-mn-18783-story.html.

———. 2020. "St. Helens: Is She Going to Sleep? Or Just Slumbering? Nobody's Sure." *Lewiston Tribune.* May 18, 2020.

https://www.lmtribune.com/premium_edition/st-helens-is-she-going
-to-sleep-or-just-slumbering-nobody-s-sure/article_349ce27b-ede2-550c
-b27d-24132aa4878d.html.

Bonnie, Hannah. 2017. "Survivors of the Mount St. Helens Eruption Tell
Their Story." *Portland Monthly*. October 12, 2017. pdxmonthly.com/arts
-and-culture/2017/10/survivors-of-the-mount-st-helens-eruption-tell-their
-story.

Brantly, Steve, and Bobbie Myers. n.d. "Mount St. Helens—From the
1980 Eruption to 2000, Fact Sheet 036–00." Accessed July 18, 2022.
pubs.usgs.gov/fs/2000/fs036-00/.

Brugman, Mindy. 2022. Personal Interview with Mindy Brugman.

Bush, Evan. 2016. "How The Seattle Times Covered the Mount St. Helens
Eruption in 1980." *Seattle Times*. May 18, 2016. seattletimes.com/seattle
-news/northwest/how-the-seattle-times-covered-the-mount-st-helens
-eruption-36-years-ago/.

Camden, Jim. 2010. "Morning Stop Gave Mount St. Helens Watchers Vital
Minutes: Researcher, Husband Barely Escaped Blast." *The Spokesman-
Review*. May 19, 2010. spokesman.com/stories/2010/may/18/morning-stop
-gave-mount-st-helens-watchers-vital-m/.

Carroll, Megan, and Destiny Johnson. 2020. "Mount St. Helens Eruption: A
Timeline in the Northwest." Krem.Com. May 7, 2020. krem.com/article
/news/local/mt-st-helens/mount-st-helens-eruption-timeline-northwest
/293-28b036fd-d7c5-4285-8d7c-4c7be2dce468.

"Coldwater Peak." n.d. Peakbagger. Accessed April 10, 2022. peakbagger.com
/peak.aspx?pid=2349.

Cornwall, Warren. 2020. "Mount St. Helens 40 Years Later: What We've
Learned, and Still Don't Know." May 18, 2020. science.org/content
/article/ecologist-has-been-studying-mount-st-helens-it-erupted-40-years
-ago.

Crisafulli, Charlie. 2015. *Charlie Crisafulli Oral History Interview*. scarc.library
.oregonstate.edu/omeka/items/show/35337.

Deshais, Nicholas. 2020. "40 Years After Mount St. Helens, Sounds of Past

Government Response Echo Today." *Northwest News Network.* May 17, 2020. nwnewsnetwork.org/disasters-and-accidents/2020-05-17/40 -years-after-mount-st-helens-sounds-of-past-government-response-echo -today.

Deviant Studios 97. 2022. "Mt. St. Helens: Dorothy Stoffel." youtu.be /tHe9E0_9RaQ?si=j0qpHPAujlsb-LIn.

Doughton, Sandi. 2009. "'Rocky' Crandell, A Giant in Northwest Volcanology." *Seattle Times.* April 10, 2009. seattletimes.com/seattle-news /rocky-crandell-a-giant-in-northwest-volcanology/.

Driedger, Carolyn. 2015. "35 Years After the Eruption: Living with the Legacy of Mount St. Helens." Washington Trails Association. May 2015. wta.org/news/magazine/features/after-the-eruption-living-with-the -legacy-of-mount-st-helens.

———. 2021. "Mount St. Helens Revisited: Lives Changed, Lessons Learned, and Legacies of the 1980 Eruptions." June 24. d9-wret.s3.us-west-2 .amazonaws.com/assets/palladium/production/s3fs-public/atoms/video /USGS%20Public%20Lecture%20Series%20-%20June%202021.mp4.

———. 2022. Personal Interview with Carolyn Driedger.

Dundas, Zach, and Rachel Ritchie. n.d. "Mount St. Helens: Anatomy of an Eruption." *Portland Monthly.* Accessed June 16, 2022. pdxmonthly.com /travel-and-outdoors/2014/06/mount-st-helens-eruption-jun-2014.

Erickson, Kristen. 2022. "What Is a Volcano?" NASA Space Place-NASA Science for Kids. March 28, 2022. spaceplace.nasa.gov/volcanoes2/en/.

Fox, Satu. 2016. "Real Jobs: What Does a Volcanologist Do?" DK Find Out! July 28, 2016. dkfindout.com/us/explore/real-jobs-what-does -volcanologist-do/.

Fox, Stuart. 2010. "How Hot Is Lava?" Live Science. June 10, 2010. livescience .com/32643-how-hot-is-lava.html.

Foxworthy, Bruce L., and Mary Hill. n.d. "Volcanic Eruptions of 1980 at Mount St. Helens: The First 100 Days." Accessed April 30, 2022. pubs .usgs.gov/pp/1249/report.pdf.

Gorney, Cynthia. 1980. "A Stifling Darkness Descended." *Washington Post,*

May 25, 1980. www.washingtonpost.com/archive/politics/1980/05/25/a
-stifling-darkness-descended/c2c09196-d4f1-4674-aa5e-00bcb56d3784/.

Guzzo, Louis R. 1980. *Is It True What They Say About Dixy?* Mercer Island,
Washington: The Writing Works, Inc.

Holmes, Melanie. 2019. *A Hero on Mount St. Helens: The Life & Legacy of
David A. Johnston.* Urbana, Illinois: University of Illinois Press.

"Holocene Activity Prior to May 18, 1980 Eruption." n.d. U.S. Geological
Survey. Accessed June 19, 2022. usgs.gov/volcanoes/mount-st.-helens
/holocene-activity-prior-may-18-1980-eruption.

"How Far Did the Ash from Mount St. Helens Travel?" n.d. U.S. Geological
Survey. Accessed June 16, 2022. usgs.gov/faqs/how-far-did-ash-mount-st
-helens-travel.

Hunter, Dana. 2012a. "Prelude to a Catastrophe: 'The Unusual Character
of the Seismic Activity Became Clear.'" *Scientific American: Rosetta
Stones* (blog). June 14, 2012. blogs.scientificamerican.com/rosetta-stones
/prelude-to-a-catastrophe-the-unusual-character-of-the-seismic-activity
-became-clear/.

———. 2012b. "Prelude to a Catastrophe: 'Something Dramatic.'" *Scientific
American: Rosetta Stones.* June 21, 2012. blogs.scientificamerican.com
/rosetta-stones/something-dramatic/.

———. 2012c. "Prelude to a Catastrophe: 'Pale-Blue Flames.'" *Scientific
American: Rosetta Stones* (blog). July 7, 2012. blogs.scientificamerican
.com/rosetta-stones/prelude-to-a-catastrophe-pale-blue-flames/.

———. 2012d. "Prelude to a Catastrophe: 'Our Best Judgement of Risk.'"
Scientific American: Rosetta Stones. July 26, 2012. blogs.scientificamerican
.com/rosetta-stones/prelude-to-a-catastrophe-our-best-judgement-of-risk/.

———. 2012e. "Prelude to a Catastrophe: 'The Volcano Could Be Nearing a
Major Event.'" *Scientific American: Rosetta Stones.* August 2, 2012. blogs
.scientificamerican.com/rosetta-stones/prelude-to-a-catastrophe-the
-volcano-could-be-nearing-a-major-event/.

———. n.d. "The Cataclysm: 'Vancouver! Vancouver! This Is It!'"
Scientific American: Blog Network. Accessed February 4, 2022. blogs

.scientificamerican.com/rosetta-stones/the-cataclysm-vancouver-vancouver
-this-is-it/.

"Interactive Map of Mount St. Helens Eruption Victims." 2010. *The Columbian*. May 18, 2010. columbian.com/news/2010/may/18/interactive
-map-mount-st-helens-eruption-victims/.

Jenkins, Austin. 2020. "At Age 6, He and His Classmates Fled Mount St. Helens. 40 Years Later This Reporter Recalls That Day." Northwest News Network. May 15, 2020. kuow.org/stories/at-age-6-he-and-his-classmates
-fled-mount-st-helens-40-years-later-this-reporter-recalls-that-day.

Jenkins, Brian. n.d. "Coldwater Peak: Climbing, Hiking & Mountaineering." SummitPost. Accessed April 10, 2022. summitpost.org/coldwater-peak
/520090.

Kafentizis, John. 1980. "Sneaking a 'Peak.'" *The Spokesman-Review*, March 28, 1980, 97 edition. news.google.com/newspapers?id=yvtLAAAAIBAJ&pg
=6950%2C6305315.

Kean, Sam. 2018. "Harry Versus the Volcano." Science History Institute. December 12, 2018. sciencehistory.org/distillations/harry-versus-the
-volcano.

Kershner, Jim. n.d. "40 Years Ago at Mount St. Helens: Harmonic Tremor Warns of Potential Huge Blast." *The Spokesman-Review*. Accessed July 17, 2022. spokesman.com/stories/2020/mar/29/40-years-ago-at-mount-st
-helens-harmonic-tremor-wa/.

KGW News, dir. 1980. *Mount St. Helens March 27, 1980: 52 Days Until the Eruption*. youtube.com/watch?v=RiwuV9oqn54.

———. dir. 2020. *Mount St. Helens, March 28, 1980. 51 Days Before the Eruption*. youtube.com/watch?v=qijA9hHofJk.

Kieffer, Susan Werner. n.d. "The Blast at Mount St. Helens: What Happened?" *CalTech Engineering & Science*. Accessed June 18, 2022. calteches.library.caltech.edu/526/2/Kieffer.pdf.

Korosec, Michael A., James G. Rigby, and Keith L. Stoffel. 1980. "The 1980 Eruption of Mount St. Helens, Washington March 20–May 19, 1980." *Information Circular* 71 (June): 19.

Krippner, Janine. 2022. Personal Interview with Janine Krippner.

———. n.d. "Remembering the Mount Saint Helens 1980 Eruption: 35 Years Later." Accessed April 19, 2022. inthecompanyofvolcanoes.blogspot.com /2015/05/remembering-mount-saint-helens-1980.html.

"Lahars Move Rapidly Down Valleys Like Rivers of Concrete." n.d. U.S. Geological Survey. Accessed April 3, 2022. usgs.gov/programs/VHP /lahars-move-rapidly-down-valleys-rivers-concrete.

"Lakes and Drainages Around Mount St. Helens." n.d. U.S. Geological Survey. Accessed May 7, 2022. usgs.gov/volcanoes/mount-st.-helens/lakes -and-drainages-around-mount-st-helens.

Leman, Jennifer. 2021. "The Hottest Temperature on Earth Was Recorded in Death Valley Last Year." *Popular Mechanics*. September 15, 2021. popularmechanics.com/science/environment/a30270365/hottest-place-on -earth/.

Major, Jon. 2022. Personal Interview with Jon Major.

Malone, Steve. 2022a. Personal Interview with Steve Malone Pt 1.

———. 2022b. Personal Interview with Steve Malone Pt 2.

Moral, Roger del. n.d. "Life Returns to Mount St. Helens." Accessed May 10, 2022. faculty.washington.edu/moral/publications/1981%20RDM%20 NH%20small.pdf.

"Mount St. Helens." 2018. History. May 9, 2018. history.com/topics/natural -disasters-and-environment/mount-st-helens.

"Mount St. Helens—Frequently Asked Questions." n.d. Pacific Northwest Research Station-US Forest Service. Accessed June 16, 2022. fs.usda.gov /research/pnw/projects/mountsthelens#faq.

"Mount St. Helens—Lateral Blast." n.d. National Geophysical Data Center-NOAA. Accessed June 16, 2022. ngdc.noaa.gov/hazard/stratoguide /helenfeat.html.

"Mount St. Helens, 1980 to Now—What's Going On?" n.d. U.S. Geological Survey and the U.S. Forest Service—Our Volcanic Public Lands. Accessed May 11, 2022. pubs.usgs.gov/fs/2013/3014/fs2013-3014_text.pdf.

"Mount St. Helens Fact Sheet." 2017. Volcano World. June 2, 2017. volcano .oregonstate.edu/mount-st-helens-fact-sheet.

"Mount St. Helens National Volcanic Monument." n.d. U.S. Geological Survey. Accessed July 18, 2022. pubs.usgs.gov/gip/msh/monument.html.

"Obituary for Donal Ray Mullineaux." n.d. Stork-Bullock Mortuary. Accessed May 11, sbmortuary.com/obituary/Donal-Mullineaux.

Olson, Steve. 2016. *Eruption: The Untold Story of Mount St. Helens.* W. W. Norton & Company.

Overstreet, Audrey. 2019. "In the Eye of Mount St. Helens: Spokane Couple Was Flying Above Volcano's Eruption on May 18, 1980." *The Spokesman-Review*, December 21, 2019. spokesman.com/stories/2019/dec/21/in-the-eye-of-mount-st-helens-spokane-couple-was-f/.

Parchman, Frank. n.d. *Echoes of Fury: The 1980 Eruption of Mount St. Helens and the Lives It Changed Forever.* Epicenter Press.

Paulson, Tom. 2005. "Mount St. Helens Still Shrouded in Secrets." *Seattle Post-Intelligencer.* May 18, 2005. seattlepi.com/seattlenews/article/Mount-St-Helens-still-shrouded-in-secrets-1173652.php.

Perry, Douglas. 2020. "Mount St. Helens Eruption: Witnesses Recall Terror, Awe When Mountain Exploded." Oregon Live. May 18, 2020. oregonlive.com/pacific-northwest-news/2020/05/mount-st-helens-eruption-witnesses-recall-terror-awe-when-mountain-exploded-40-years-ago.html.

"Pyroclastic Flows Move Fast and Destroy Everything in Their Path." n.d. U.S. Geological Survey. Accessed April 3, 2022. usgs.gov/programs/VHP/pyroclastic-flows-move-fast-and-destroy-everything-their-path.

"Reid Blackburn." n.d. National Press Photographers Foundation. Accessed April 6, 2022. nppf.org/scholarship-bios/reid-blackburn/.

Robinson, Erik. 2010. "A Race to Survive: Sunday Morning Drive Turns into Frantic Trip to Escape Eruption." *The Columbian.* April 1, 2010. columbian.com/news/2010/apr/01/survivors-a-race-with-death/.

Robson, Sarah. 2022. "What We Know About the Tonga Eruption, Four Months On." RNZ. May 13, 2022. rnz.co.nz/programmes/the-detail/story/2018841825/what-we-know-about-the-tonga-eruption-four-months-on.

Rose, Robert L. 1980. "Washington Volcano Blowing Its Top: St. Helens Burps Out Ash, Smoke." *The Spokesman-Review*, March 28, 1980. news.google.com/newspapers?id=yvtLAAAAIBAJ&pg=6950%2C6305315.

Saarinen, Thomas F., and James L. Sell. 1985. *Warning and Response to the Mount St. Helen's Eruption*. Albany, NY: State University of New York Press.

Schlom, Dave, and Matt Fidler. 2020. "Blue Dot 179: A BLAST FROM THE PAST: Mt St. Helens 40 Years Ago With Donald Swanson." NSPR. May 15, 2020. mynspr.org/show/blue-dot/2020-05-15/blue-dot-179-a-blast -from-the-past-mt-st-helens-40-years-ago-with-donald-swanson.

Scientist Killed in Mount St. Helens Eruption Remembered 40 Years After Deadly Blast. 2020. king5.com/article/tech/science/environment/mount -st-helens/david-johnston-mount-st-helens-eruption/281-81d2a420-5a0c -4dbc-ad61-ca06e5c7f11c.

Spencer, Keith. "Spirit Lake, the holder of a dark secret," *The Spokesman-Review*. October 11, 2007. spokesman.com/stories/2007/oct/11/spirit-lake -the-holder-of-a-dark-secret/.

"St. Helens Hero-David Johnston." n.d. Accessed February 6, 2022. sthelenshero.com/DavidJohnston.html.

Stricherz, Vince. 2000. "Twenty Years after Big Blast: Mount St. Helens Leaves Legacy of More Accurate Eruption Predictions." *UW News* (blog). April 24, 2000. washington.edu/news/2000/04/24/twenty -years-after-big-blast-mount-st-helens-leaves-legacy-of-more-accurate -eruption-predictions/.

———. 2010. "Experts List: Lessons from Mount St. Helens Being Applied Today." *UW News* (blog). May 3, 2010. washington.edu/news/2010/05 /03/experts-list-lessons-from-mount-st-helens-being-applied-today/.

Taylor, Alan. 2015. "The Eruption of Mount St. Helens in 1980." *The Atlantic*. May 18, 2015. theatlantic.com/photo/2015/05/the-eruption-of-mount-st -helens-in-1980/393557/.

"The Sound, or Silence, of an Erupting Volcano." n.d. Stylus WBUR ILab. Accessed July 8, 2022. stylusradio.org/post/80549530367/the-sound-or -silence-of-an-erupting-volcano-on.

"Then and Now: The Mount St. Helens Eruption, Four Decades Later." 2020. *College of the Environment, University of Washington* (blog). May 18,

2020. environment.uw.edu/news/2020/05/then-and-now-the-mount-st
-helens-eruption-four-decades-later.

Thompson, Dick. n.d. *Volcano Cowboys: The Rocky Evolution of a Dangerous Science*. New York, N.Y: Thomas Dunne Books.

Tobin, Harold. 2022. Personal Interview with Harold Tobin.

"USGS Photographic Library Explorer." n.d. Accessed February 8, 2022. library.usgs.gov/photo/#/?terms=david%20johnston.

Vogt, Tom. 2018. "'We Had Our Tent and Sleeping Bags out of the Car.'" *The Columbian*. May 18, 2018. columbian.com/news/2018/may/18 /hydrologist-recalls-life-saving-advice-mount-st-helens-may-18-1980/.

———. n.d. "Waking to a Nightmare." *The Columbian*. Accessed April 16, 2022. columbian.com/news/2010/apr/01/survivors-waking-to-a-nightmare/.

"Volcano Watch—25 Years Later, What Have We Learned from Mount St. Helens?" n.d. U.S. Geological Survey. Accessed August 23, 2022. usgs .gov/news/volcano-watch-25-years-later-what-have-we-learned-mount-st -helens.

"Volcano Watch—How High Is That Lava Fountain?" U.S. Geological Survey, Hawaiian Volcano Observatory. October 28, 2021. usgs.gov/news /volcano-watch-how-high-lava-fountain.

Waitt, Richard. n.d. *In the Path of Destruction: Eyewitness Chronicles of Mount St. Helens*.

Washington National Guard, dir. 2017. *News Piece on Guard's Response During Mt. St. Helens*. youtube.com/watch?v=-NipLKNIXG0.

"Where Do Earthquakes Happen?" n.d. Michigan Technological University. Accessed November 3, 2022. mtu.edu/geo/community/seismology/learn /earthquake-location/.

"Who Was David Johnston?" n.d. U.S. Geological Survey. Accessed February 6, 2022. legistorm.com/stormfeed/view_rss/261797/organization/35286/title /who-was-david-johnston-us-geological-survey-press-release-legistorm.html.